Beloved

Faith Maker

The Believer's Manual

Ruth van Vliet

Beloved Faith Maker

ISBN-13: 978-0-620-86282-0

Copyright © 2019 by Ruth van Vliet
All rights reserved

Email-Address: ruth@heroic.co.za
Web Address: www.heroic.co.za

1st Printing of Hardcopy February 2020

Published by **Christ in us Ministries Trust, trading as Heroic**
Web Address: heroic.co.za

Cover design was done by Bianca van Vliet, Copyright ©2019.
Manuscript prepared for Publication by **Publication Movement International LLC**
Web Address: www.publishing-movement.com

All rights reserved under International Copyright Law.
Contents may not be reproduced in whole or in part in any form without the express written consent of the publisher.

Unless otherwise indicated, all Scripture quotations are from The ESV® Bible (the Holy Bible, English Standard Version®), Copyright © 2001 by Crossway, a publishing ministry of Good News Publishers. Used by permission. All rights reserved.

Scripture quotations marked GW are taken from God's Word, Copyright © 1995 by GOD'S WORD to the Nations Bible Society. Quotations are used by permission. All rights reserved.

Scripture quotations marked ISV are taken from the International Standard Version® Release 2.0. Copyright © 1996-2010 by the ISV Foundation. Used by permission of Davidson Press, LLC. All rights reserved.

All emphasis or explanations given in brackets, capitalizations or additional punctuation within Scripture quotations, are the author's own.

Thank you

A special thank you to Eksderde and to Apostolic Movement International.

With sincere thanks and honour to all who taught me in the Word and in the fellowship of the Holy Spirit. Thank you for your teachings, mentoring and leadership. Thanks for pouring out all you had to give. Your selfless love for the Lord and His people inspired me so much. I couldn't have done this without you.

With sincere thanks to my husband Arie and children Bianca, Eloise and Sebastian. Thank you for your grace and your love. I love you.

Contents

Part 1 9
Introduction 9
Chapter 1 What Is This Book About?...10
    Redefining a Manual 10
    The Love of a Bride 11
    Watching a Movie 12
    The Whole Bible 13
    Preaching Christ from the Old Testament......................................14
    What's Next 16
Part 2 17
Connecting with God's Heart from Genesis to Revelation................17
Chapter 2 From the Beginning...18
    Adam and Eve Didn't Have a Bible..19
    Three Things That Stop God's Blessings......................................20
    Faith Captivates God's Heart 21
    The Scriptures Give Instruction, Encouragement, and Hope 22
    The Relationship between Hope and Faith....................................23
    God's Unshakeable Beacon of Hope to All Nations 24
    What Does "Believe" Mean? 26
Chapter 3 God Led Israel Out of Egypt and Into the Promised Land..........29

Why Did God Choose Israel as His People? 29
What about the Gentiles? 30
Signs Were Given That All May Believe and Know That He Is God......30
God's Covenant with Israel, and God's Warning 31
God's GLORY 32
God Wanted to Live Amongst His People, to Be With Them, Lead Them, and Love Them...32
Circumcised Hearts 33
Jesus, the Messiah, Prophesied in the Wilderness...................................36
Moses' Last Instructions to the People of Israel 37
Joshua Leads the People into Canaan and Divides the Land 41

Chapter 4 The Period When the Judges Led God's People 43
Why Did God Appoint Judges?...43
Grace for Ruth Also 45
Samuel (1060 – 1020 BC)..45

Chapter 5 Israel's First Three Kings 47
The Lord Anointed Saul to Be King (1051 – 1011 BC)..........................48
Why Was David Chosen by God to be Anointed as King?.....................49
God's Covenant with David..54
David's Mistakes...54
David's Instructions to Solomon 55
King Solomon (971 – 931 BC)...56
The Lord's Promise That He Will Always Be Available in the Temple ..57
The Lord's Earnest Warning to Solomon..58
Solomon Did Not Walk in the Way of the Gift of Wisdom 58

Chapter 6 What Did Kings David and Solomon Write About? 61
Psalms 62
1. David's Secret to Success..62
2. Some Messianic Prophecies in Psalms..63
David's Songs About God's Thoughts on Mankind 68
Proverbs - The Way of Wisdom..69
Ecclesiastes 71

Song of Solomon 72
Chapter 7 The Divided Kingdom, Prophets Jonah, Amos and Hosea 74
    A Summary of the Kings of Israel (931BC to 722BC) 78
    A Summary of the Kings of Judah (931BC – 586 BC) 79
    The Lord's Prophets 82
    Jonah (781 BC) 83
    Amos (765-754 BC) 85
    Hosea (758-725 BC) 88
Chapter 8 Prophets Isaiah and Micah 92
    God Declares an "End" and a "New Thing" Through Prophet Isaiah (760 - 673 BC) 92
    One Night 92
    The Lord's Sorrow 93
    The Lord Earnestly Reassures That He Is Trustworthy 96
    The Messiah 100
    God's Victory Over Sin Decreed 106
    Other Guidance From the Lord 113
    God's Plan 114
    Micah (738-698 BC) 116
Chapter 9 Prophets Jeremiah, Ezekiel and Zephaniah 118
    Jeremiah (650-582 BC) 118
    False Prophets 119
    The Condition of the Lord's People 121
    How the Lord Pleaded With His People 126
    The Outcome of Judah's Faithlessness and the Future Hope 127
    Ezekiel (620 – 570 BC) 131
    Because They Defiled His Intimate Sanctuary 131
    God's Glory Left the Temple 135
    Empowered to Obey 135
    The Lord's Covenant of Peace 139
    Zephaniah (640 – 626 BC) 142
Chapter 10 Job 145

- Having Conversations about God, or With God?....................145
- Chapter 11 The Remaining Books of the Old Testament..........151
  - Nahum (658 – 615 BC)..151
  - Daniel (620 – 540 BC)..152
  - Obadiah (590 BC)...155
  - Habakkuk (608 – 598 BC)...155
  - Haggai (520 BC)...157
  - Zechariah (522 – 509 BC)..157
  - Ezra and Nehemiah (538 – 430 BC)................................158
  - Esther (478 BC)...159
  - Malachi (465 BC)..159
  - Joel (450 BC)...161
  - The Promised Anointing: The "New" of God's Kingdom..........163
- Chapter 12 God's Kingdom...165
  - The Time Has Come!..165
  - Jesus' Bride...170
- Part 3..174
- How to Reign with Christ in Ordinary, Everyday Life................174
- Chapter 13 Doing Life With God...175
  - Feed on Jesus..175
  - The Genuineness of Your Faith......................................177
  - Supplement Your Faith...178
  - LAUGH..179
  - Transformation...182
  - Grace is Your Trainer...183
- Chapter 14 Training in Virtue..184
  - Being Genuine..184
  - As a Child...185
- Chapter 15 Training in Godliness by the Holy Spirit................190
  - Being Led by the Holy Spirit.......................................190
  - 1. Do God's Plan Rather Than Your Own Plan......................194

    2. The Voice of the Enemy 194

    3. What is Deception? 196

    4. The Lord's Voice 196

    5. The Voice of Your Own Mind 198

    6. The Voice of Your Own Heart 199

    7. When Do You Know That You Are in God's Will? 199

    8. When God Is Too Quiet 200

    9. How to Ensure That Prophecy Is of the Lord 200

    10. Your Authority 201

Chapter 16 Training in Brotherly Affection and Love 206

    Love 206

    God's Glory in Marriage 218

    God's Glory in Parenting 220

    Conclusion 222

Recommended Resources 226

Part 1

Introduction

What Is This Book About?

Redefining a Manual

This book is not an ordinary manual.

Years ago, I went back to working as a programmer in Information Technology after I had been out of the industry for about 18 years. My new boss gave me a set of manuals and a computer, and most of the time I had to figure things out by trial and error.

Furthermore, I had to adjust to long hours in traffic, long hours at a new job, and to a different fetching-kids-from-school-and-university routine with my teenage children. Life was a tough challenge.

Every day, I relied on the Holy Spirit to help me come to grips with my new job and to cope with all the changes that were happening in my life. My new routine was very different from being a housewife, substitute teacher, and minister.

At work, the Lord truly helped me to understand the manuals and to ask my colleagues the right questions who were very helpful to point me in the right direction.

One day, one of them made a comment to someone else saying, "Ruth learned everything very quickly," to which I replied, "But I had a manual!"

Because I was feeling embarrassed and put on the spot, I used a silly accent and it came out as, "But I had Immanuel!"

The moment I heard what came out of my mouth, I felt so blessed! For yes, it was actually all about Immanuel: God was with me and He was helping me with anything and everything.

A Manual Times Two

God is very passionate about living everyday life in companionship with you. He wants to be your first go-to person and Immanuel in everything you do and experience!

Not only that, Jesus is the Word who became flesh and lived amongst people. It is written that in the beginning the Word was with God and that the Word was God - all things were created through Him (John 1:1-3&14).

Therefore, Jesus is both, Immanuel by leading you and helping you through His personal relationship with you, as well as your manual through the written Word, giving instructions and encouragement for daily life while transforming you from glory to glory.

Jesus said, *"My brothers, My sisters and My mother are those who hear the Word and do the Word; those who do the will of My Father."* (Mark 3:31-35, Luke 8:19-21 and Matthew 12:46-50)

When you are bombarded with all sorts of things from different directions at the same time and do not know which way to turn, the only solid rock and firm foundation are God's words. As you grow and mature, they anchor your soul when your mind and emotions are caught up in a tsunami on the open seas.

God's words are also the lighthouse that will bring you back to shore safely and cause you to be secure and peaceful.

The Love of a Bride

A bride longs to please her bridegroom because she loves and adores him, just as he longs to please her.

They do this not because they have to, but because they want to, for they are in love.

At the time of Esther, King Ahasuerus was looking for someone to replace queen Vashti in her royal position because she rejected him and treated him with contempt. I am sure you know the story of how Esther wanted to please the king and to ask for nothing except what the king's eunuch advised.

All the other women were interested only in what they could gain from the king. Those who were given the opportunity to spend one night with him were entitled to ask for anything from his harem, but not Esther. She found grace and favor with the king and he loved her (Esther 2:13-17).

This is the type of love that Jesus' bride has: she seeks to adore Him and to please Him only. She does everything it takes to know what pleases Him for she knows He is her Beloved. She does this not because she feels insecure or seeks to gain His approval, but she does this from a place of security and confidence in who He is and whom He made her to be.

He is her Husband, her Maker, the one who helps her to see how wide and deep His love for her is, so that she is able to have faith in His ability and intentions to love and take good care of her.

How deep is your longing to know God more intimately? The Scriptures are like the king's eunuch – giving you all the information that you need, to know Him more intimately.

You will discover what He likes and what breaks His heart. It is up to you to decide what to do with the information.

Watching a Movie

Have you ever wanted to watch a movie, but instead of watching it from the start, you started in the middle and watched for five minutes? Then, weeks later, you watch either the same five minutes again, or you watch another five or ten minutes starting from another place in the movie.

Do you think I'm nuts? Well, it would be nuts to try and watch a movie like that and follow what's going on. We don't watch movies like that, yet we often read the Bible that way.

Agreed – the Bible is much, much bigger to read, listen to, or watch in just one sitting. The struggle is real. The Bible is big and to read it all overwhelms many people.

This book is intended to help you with this dilemma as it equips you with a condensed version of events from beginning to end. It follows the books of the Old Testament chronologically up through the New Testament, so that you can watch a "movie" of the events playing off in your mind's eye while reading.

The Whole Bible

The "God of the Old Testament"

I don't know about you, but I used to be afraid to read the Old Testament. I was afraid that I would read about a God who would make me afraid of Him.

Somewhere I picked up an idea in my heart that the "God in the Old Testament" was just angry, ready to lash out, punish, and kill people.

I was over the moon when I got born again and got to know Jesus. What confused me a little, however, was that Jesus said, "If you've seen me, you've seen the Father." Also, the Apostle Paul wrote in his letter to the church in Colossae that "Jesus is the image of the invisible God" (Colossians 1:15).

So then I decided that God was not just mean, and did not get angry anymore, because He vented all His anger on Jesus when He died on the cross to take the punishment for the sins of all mankind upon Himself. I was just so happy and grateful for His grace and to know that nothing can separate me from His love.

But I still had questions. I still wanted to understand why God got so angry in the Old Testament. Then, when I discovered God's heart and how and why it happened that He was angry, everything suddenly made sense. He multiplied my faith by millions and He can do it for you.

The Law and the Veil

There is another reason why I was afraid to read the Old Testament.

I grew up in a Christian home and on Sundays, we went to church where the Ten Commandments of the Law were read during the service.

While listening to the law, I always felt that I was never going to make it and that I could never be good enough. Every time I heard "though shall not," I cringed and felt almost hopeless. During that time, I wasn't born again and I desperately tried to read my Bible and to understand God using my mind and my natural abilities. Our church (I'm not trying to offend anyone, but just giving my testimony) didn't believe that we should be born again, as we were born and raised in a Christian home. The working of the Holy Spirit wasn't taught in that church at that time.

When I was 35, by the grace of God, somebody invited me to a women's camp where I learned for the first time in my life that God wants to talk to us here and now –today – and that we don't have to wait to get to heaven to truly experience God! I was born again. For the first time in my life, I started to understand what Jesus accomplished for us on the cross and I felt reconciled with God.

After that weekend, I couldn't put my Bible down. I just wanted to know Jesus more and more and to love Him. I was over the moon with joy and had such courage. All I wanted to do was convert people and help them be born again and experience God!

Then I read in 2 Corinthians 3, about the glory that Moses had, and about the glory of the New Covenant being a greater glory than the glory of the law. When Moses came down from being on the mountain with the Lord, his face shone and it had to be covered with a veil so that he could be amongst the people. I read that, "to this day, when they read the Old Covenant, that same veil remains, because only through Christ is it taken away. To this day, when Moses is read, a veil lies over their hearts. However, when one turns to the Lord, the veil is removed. Now the Lord is the Spirit and where the Spirit of the Lord is, there is freedom".

All I could hear was, "when the law was read, the veil remained". Because I had such hurt, anger, and even rebellion in my heart (because my church didn't lead me to being born again), the fear that I would lose what I had received from the Lord – that precious gift of connection and knowing Him, of being able to see and touch Him in the Spirit – that fear was very real, and I desperately didn't want to lose it.

So I tried to avoid reading the Old Testament and when I read it, I had this wall in my heart, fearing that I would lose Jesus.

Today I know, because there is no more rebellion, hurt, fear or anger in my heart (for the Lord healed me and set me free), that the veil is removed by the Spirit of God when you are born again.

I personally gained better understanding of the scope of the mind of Christ by reading the whole Bible.

Preaching Christ from the Old Testament

Before Jesus ascended into heaven, He opened the hearts of the apostles to understand the Scriptures, where it was written about Him in the law and the prophets. This fascinated me and I longed to understand this. The apostles preached Christ from the Old Testament, teaching people that Jesus was the Messiah, the anointed one, the Christ from the Scriptures.

This book emphasizes what was written in the Scriptures about the Messiah to help you have absolute certainty that Jesus is the Christ, the Messiah, sent by God.

You will read of the reasons and the events that led up to the birth of Jesus and the outpouring of the Holy Spirit.

"Messiah" and "Christ"

"Messiah" and "Christ" have the same meaning, which is "anointed".

- "Messiah" is from the Hebrew word meaning "anointed"
- "Christ" is from the Greek word meaning "anointed"

God spoke through the law and the prophets about the coming Messiah, whom He called His anointed, His branch, His servant, His shepherd, His son, or the offspring of David, whose kingdom will be an everlasting kingdom.

"Zion"

"Zion" is a word that is used a number of times especially in the Old Testament. It refers to a place where God lives (Psalm 132:13).

Of old, it referred to a mountain in Jerusalem where the temple of the Lord was built and where He graced them with His presence.

In referring to the new, spiritual kingdom of God, I believe that "Zion" refers to believers in Jesus Christ, being built up together as a spiritual house and temple where the Lord lives (Hebrews 12:22, 1 Peter 2:4-25).

Through Two or Three Witnesses

A principle that God uses quite frequently is that He establishes truth through two or three witnesses. This universal principle is referred to in the Law of Moses, by Jesus, and by Paul (Deuteronomy 17:6, 19:15, Matthew 18:16, 2 Corinthians 13:1).

You will find that many of the prophets confirm God's decrees and prophecies, albeit in different words, shapes, and forms.

Jesus came and fulfilled every single one of the numerous prophecies that God declared about Him as the Messiah.

It is also great to notice phrases from the Old Testament that are used (not necessarily quoted) in the New Testament. Paul was especially good at this as he wrote, for example, about bitterness and boasting in his letters to believers. These phrases make a lovely thread through the Bible, woven by the Holy Spirit, to tie all the books of the Bible together as a whole.

What's Next

Part 2 of this book takes you on a journey of faith and personal transformation through the Word as you connect with God's heart from Genesis to Revelation, while watching the "movie".

All I can say is that I am not the same person I was since I've started working on this book.

I thought I was okay until I read, and read, and read the Word. While I was reading, God was doing something in me. He was adding, removing, shaping, polishing, confronting, and revealing.

I re-read and re-wrote many times more and asked the Lord if I was ever going to complete this book.

His answer was, "Ruth, I want you to understand the process of transformation. My Word is meant to make you new, by washing away what shouldn't be part of you, and by planting and watering what needs to develop and grow."

The bottom line is that God wants you to be able to have complete faith in who He is, knowing what He did and why, and also to have faith that He made and equipped you with everything you need to live the life that He intended for you to live.

Part 3 gives you the "1-2-3" of how to live in faith and reign with Christ every day of your life, built on the way and the foundation that God revealed and established in His Word (Part 2).

 Glory to Glory Q&A

1. What are you currently trusting God for in your life?
2. What scripture, prophecy, or personal word has the Lord given you regarding this promise?
3. Who told you about Father God, Jesus, and the Holy Spirit?
4. Who gave you your first Bible?
5. How certain are you that God is the one and only true, living God?
   Rate your confidence in who God is, on a scale of 1 to 10, with 1 being very uncertain about who God is, and 10 being absolutely certain about who God is.

Part 2

Connecting with God's Heart from Genesis to Revelation

Chapter 2

From the Beginning

All God Ever Wanted

All God ever wanted to do was to love you.

All God ever wanted to be was your companion and your Savior.

He always wanted to be the one to fight for you, and the one who helps you.

He always wanted to be the one who takes care of you, laughs with you, and cries with you.

He always intended for you to hear His voice and to listen to His voice as He guides you through the landmines of evil in the world, so that you are protected from harm, and led in the way of peace, growth, and blessing.

At the Beginning of His Work

What do expecting parents normally do? They are usually dreaming and making plans for the baby that they are expecting! They are probably imagining if it's a boy or a girl, and who they will look like. They also plan the nursery. They buy a cot, a pram, a car seat, clothes, nappies and whatever is needed for the baby to live life!

Well, before God made the earth and everything in it, He was so excited about you! What He did in six days creating the universe and everything in it was actually the biggest baby shower of all time!

He created the heavens and the earth to experience it with you! The sun, the stars, the whole universe, the moonlight, the sunsets, the flowers, Africa's big five, the sea, the solar eclipse – you name it!

I have such fond memories of my dad, sharing the first peach, or the first radish, of the season from his vegetable garden. He would divide them into five pieces, so that each one in the family could savor and taste its freshness. I believe it was exactly as Father God intended for us to taste and savor this beautiful life that He has given us!

Proverbs 8:22-31
> The Lord possessed me (wisdom) at the beginning of His work, the first of His acts of old. Ages ago I was set up, at the first, before the beginning of the earth. When there were no depths I was brought forth, when there were no springs abounding with water.
>
> Before the mountains had been shaped, before the hills, I was brought forth, before He had made the earth with its fields, or the first of the dust of the world.
>
> When He established the heavens, I was there; when He drew a circle on the face of the deep, when He made firm the skies above, when He established the fountains of the deep, when He assigned to the sea its limit, so that the waters might not transgress His command, when He marked out the foundations of the earth, then I was beside Him, like a master workman, and I was daily His delight, rejoicing before Him always, rejoicing in His inhabited world and delighting in the children of man.

What a beautiful masterpiece He created for us! He meticulously thought of everything to keep this earth intact for you and I to enjoy and to live in. He planned the circle of life, the water cycle, the nitrogen cycle, and the tides of the sea – everything in the universe so that we could have a sustainable planet to live on!

Why? Because God loves us.

Not only that, I think He wanted to brag a bit about how magnificent He is – like a lover wanting to impress the love of his life, or like a Father wanting to bless His children far beyond anything that they could pray or think!

Adam and Eve Didn't Have a Bible

Adam and Eve didn't know if they could trust God, or the enemy.

They chose to believe the snake instead of believing that **God** was the one telling them the truth, warning them not to eat of the fruit that will cause their death!

They had absolutely no frame of reference as to what the **consequences** of listening to the devious voice of the enemy would be, and they chose to disobey God.

They had no Bible to read to point them in the right direction.

Neither was there anyone else to ask, "Can we trust God?"

"Why would God want to warn us?"

They had no one to say, "Be careful – the devil is a liar and a thief! He has been a murderer and a destroyer since the beginning (John 8:44)! He prowls around to see whom he can devour (1 Peter 5:8)!"

We have the privilege to have an ocean of testimonies and warnings, should we be wise and humble enough to take notice.

Three Things That Stop God's Blessings

As you follow the events through the Bible, you will notice a pattern of three main things in the hearts of people that stopped God's blessings in their lives:

1) Unbelief
   (Hebrews 3:19, Matthew 13:58, Romans 11:20,23)
2) Disobedience
   (Hebrews 4:6, Ephesians 2:1-2)
3) A hardened heart filled with stubbornness, rebellion and pride
   (Hebrews 3:7-12, 1 Peter 5:5, James 4:6, Luke 1:51-53)

Adam and Eve didn't believe God, but they believed the devil. They didn't obey God, but they obeyed the one who wanted to destroy God's plan for their lives. Unbelief and disobedience go hand in hand with a hardened heart. Pride (the flesh, actually) always wants to rule and be God.

Why the Flood?

The slap in the face that God received from Adam and Eve was sadly only the first of so many that mankind would hand out to Him! They kicked Him, spat in His face and rejected Him over, and over, and over again, and still He forgave them and had mercy on them, because His steadfast love endures forever.

There was a time, not long after Adam and Eve, when God was pushed beyond His limits for the thoughts in the minds of the people were continually evil, and it grieved Him to His heart, and He regretted that He had made man on earth. That was when He sent the flood and saved Noah and his family (Genesis 6:5-8).

Beginning to End

From beginning to end, the Bible tells story after story of people choosing evil above His goodness, blatantly rejecting His love and His voice to pursue the most atrocious evil, with horrible consequences.

Fortunately, from beginning to end, the Bible also tells of the glorious blessings poured out on those who believed God and trusted in Him. It tells the stories of how He fought their battles for them, healed them, and even raised the dead!

Over and over and over again, God proved His faithfulness, mercy, steadfast love, and the magnificence of His power to fight for those He loves.

One thing I know beyond a shadow of a doubt: God has given His everything to make known to mankind how much He loves them, and what lengths He would go to, to make them say, "I do. I do believe you, Lord. I trust You."

Faith Captivates God's Heart

Song of Solomon 4:9
> You have captivated My heart, My sister, My bride; **you have captivated My heart with one glance of your eyes,** with one jewel of your necklace.

When you glance to God for help, and you put your faith and trust in Him, it totally ravishes His heart. Our faith in Him is an expression of our love towards Him, and it makes His knees weak like nothing else in all creation can.

- God is the only person who will ever understand all the pictures in your life, for He has always been with you.
- There is no one else who could ever know you like He does.
- There is no one else in all creation who could ever love you like He does.

All He ever wanted was to take care of His people and to bless them. The very first thing that God did after creating Adam was to bless him (Genesis 1:26-28).

What was the first thing that God did after Adam and Eve sinned? God gave them the redemption plan for their sin - that the woman's seed, Christ, would crush the head and authority of satan!

Right through the Bible, God "cleaned up" the messes His people made. Christ's death on the cross is a prime example of that. The Son of God paid the final penalty for sins, once and for all, and was bruised, killed, and punished for the transgressions of the world according to the will of God! Why was it God's will for Jesus to be crucified? It was so that He could make many to be accounted righteous – that is, to be in right standing with God, justified and reconciled with God.

The Value of Seeing the Consequences of the Three Things That Stop God

At first, Adam and Eve didn't comprehend the huge value of God's warning not to eat of the forbidden fruit. Before their fall, they didn't understand what God was talking about when He warned them about evil. Their frame of reference was very limited.

When you really start to notice the consequences of unbelief, disobedience, and a hardened heart, then you can truly understand why to pursue goodness. Then you will want to obey God's voice with your whole heart and with everything you've got.

The Scriptures Give Instruction, Encouragement, and Hope

Romans 15:4
> For whatever was written in former days was written for our **instruction**, that through **endurance** and through the **encouragement** of the Scriptures we might have **hope**.

The Scriptures encourage us to have **hope**:

God proves Himself to be <u>faithful</u> over and over again. When Joshua led Israel into the Promised Land after Moses had passed on, He said in Joshua 21:45, "Not one word of all the good promises that the LORD had made to the house of Israel had failed; all came to pass."

The promises that God made in the Scriptures give us hope as an anchor, for God told the prophet Jeremiah that, "I am watching over My word to perform it (Jeremiah 1:12)."

Abraham against hope in hope believed that God would give him a son in old age, for he knew that God is faithful, and He does what He says (Romans 4:18-21).

Because of Israel's unbelief and rebellion against God, it took them 40 years to enter the Promised Land. Nevertheless, God kept His promise and He led them into the Promised Land. Of the millions of people who left Egypt, only two people (Caleb and Joshua) entered the Promised Land because they believed God. The others perished in the desert.

Abraham waited 24 years until Isaac was born, his promised son and heir.

How long have you been waiting for your promises to be fulfilled?

Through the encouragement found in the Scriptures that God is faithful and will deliver on His promises, we are empowered to persevere with endurance having faith in God until the fulfillment of the promises.

The Relationship between Hope and Faith

Hebrews 11:1
> Now **faith** is the <u>assurance</u> of things **hoped** for, the <u>conviction</u> of things **not seen**.

So, faith has to do with the fulfillment of things hoped for.

It is really key to <u>test</u> what you hope for and trust God for!

- Regarding the Promised Land, did Israel build their faith and hope in a word and promises received from God, or in a sensual desire of the flesh?
- Regarding Isaac, did Abraham build his hope on a promise received from God, or on a good idea he had one morning?

Believe me, you will be saved a lot of heartache, blood, sweat, and tears the day you realize to put your hope and faith in God's voice and His promises and … nothing else, actually.

Test what you've put your faith and hope into. Is it based on God's Word and His values and principles? Remember, the enemy even twists God's Word. He even tried to tempt Jesus using scriptures, but Jesus was smarter, for He knew the context of what was written!

I've had many struggles where the enemy twisted God's Word and I fell for it. If it wasn't for the counsel I received from my spiritual leaders, I would have gone astray really badly. Thank goodness we have a Bible and the body of Christ to support us.

See? God wasn't making any mistakes. He knew exactly what He had to put into place for the body of Christ to function, as He was developing and growing it!

Everything happens for a reason and works together for good.

God's Unshakeable Beacon of Hope to All Nations

From the start, God set an unshakable beacon of hope for all nations, by His promise to Abraham. The hope was that God would establish a way for all nations to partake in His blessings.

1. God's Promise to All Believers

After God had called Abram and sent him out to a land that He would point out to him, He blessed Abram, saying that in him all the generations and families of the earth will be blessed.

The scriptures confirm God's promise to Abraham seven times (Genesis 12:2-3,7; 13:14-16;15:4-5,18;17:4-8;22:16-18)!

God also confirmed the promise with an oath, which makes this promise rock solid, unmovable and unchangeable, so that all who put their faith in this hope shall not be put to shame.

God tested Abraham's faith by asking him to offer Isaac as a sacrifice. He believed that God would provide, for he knew that God could raise the dead and he obeyed without hesitation.

After the Lord provided the ram for the sacrifice in Isaac's place, the angel of the Lord said to him from heaven in Genesis 22:15-18:

> "By Myself I have sworn, declares the Lord, because you have done this and have not withheld your son, your only son, I will surely bless you, and I will surely multiply your offspring as the stars of heaven and as the sand that is on the seashore. And your offspring shall possess the gate of his enemies, and in your offspring shall ALL the nations of the earth be blessed, because you have obeyed My voice."

All through the Old Testament, God remembered and kept His promise to the physical descendants of Abraham. That is also why the gospel of Jesus Christ was first preached to the Jews, and then spread to the Gentiles. God kept His word.

Even when Abraham had Ishmael with Hagar, and she treated Sarah with contempt, Hagar cried out to the Lord and the Lord had mercy on her and blessed Ishmael. However, God's redemption plan for the world was through Isaac, because Jesus would be born from Isaac's bloodline (Genesis 21:8-21, Galatians 4:21-31).

Also, God revealed His majesty and that He is the Savior in that Abraham and Sarah conceived in old age. What is impossible with man, is possible with God. He confirmed His character of wanting to show His love by doing great deeds, what the flesh would call "against all odds".

2. Righteousness Obtained by Faith

Abraham believed God, and it was counted to him as righteousness.

"Righteousness" means to be in right standing with God; to be accepted, at peace, and justified by Him.

After God had called Abram and blessed him, he and his trained men went to rescue Lot who was living in Sodom at the time and was taken captive by a group of kings. Afterwards, Melchizedek, king of Salem, priest of the Most High God, met him and blessed him. Abraham gave him a tenth of the spoil.

Then Melchizedek served Abraham bread and wine.

Melchizedek means "king of righteousness" and Salem means "peace" (Hebrews 6,7). At this very early time in history, the law already prophesied by these actions that Jesus would come as the bread of life, and His blood as the wine, which we now know as the offering for sin, meant to establish God's righteousness and thus declaring peace and reconciliation with God.

Luke 22:19-20
> And He (Jesus) took bread, and when He had given thanks, He broke it and gave it to them, saying, "This is My body, which is given for you. Do this in remembrance of Me." And likewise the cup after they had eaten, saying, "This cup that is poured out for you is the new covenant in My blood."

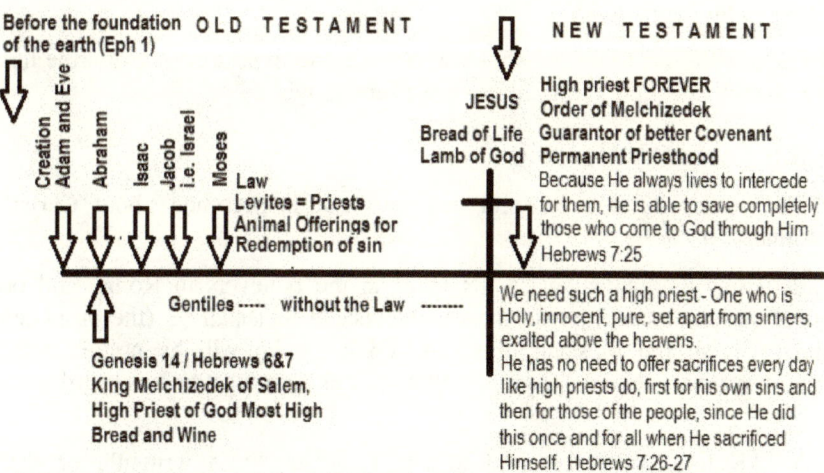

Where a change of Priesthood takes place, there must also be a change in the law (Hebrews 7:12). By God's will we have been sanctified once and for all through the sacrifice of the body of Jesus Christ (Hebrews 10:10).

In Psalm 110, David prophesied that Christ would be priest forever according to the order of Melchizedek. Melchizedek is without father or mother or genealogy, having neither beginning of days nor end of life, but resembling the Son of God, he continues as priest forever. This was long before there was either a Jacob (who became Israel) or a Levi (one of Jacob's sons) from whom the Levitical priests came according to the law of Moses.

God's hope of salvation to all who would put their faith in Jesus Christ was established, standing firm for centuries until Christ came at the appointed time.

God appointed Abraham as the father of all who believe (Romans 4).

What Does "Believe" Mean?

The definition of "believe" is to accept something as true.

However, just because you've accepted something as true, it doesn't mean that it is really true, does it?

Times of trials and testing usually reveal the state of our hearts: whether we stand firm in genuine faith and in trusting God, or whether we have stumbling blocks like doubts, fear, disappointments, uncertainty, confusion or deception that are injuring our faith.

What you believe in your heart determines how you behave, for as a man thinks in his heart, so he is.

Transformation is to refine what you believe – to expose and uproot the lies and to cultivate God's truth in our hearts and minds.

Faith Comes by Hearing

"Faith comes by hearing, and hearing what is preached about Christ" (Romans 10:17).

Paul writes this statement in his letter to the believers in Rome, and he quotes what was written by the prophet Isaiah in Isaiah 53 (the prophecy about Christ, the Messiah, the anointed one who will be crucified for transgressions), verse 1, saying, "Who has <u>believed</u> what he has <u>heard</u> from us?"

Just like Jesus often referred to scriptures as "it is written", or that "scriptures should be fulfilled", the apostle Paul also merged the wonder of the New Covenant proceedings with the law and the prophets that were written before!

All this was done to help people to have <u>hope</u>, and to be able to <u>believe</u> and to <u>trust God</u>.

Nothing builds faith more than knowing God's faithfulness to His Word.

- **If the Word is a lamp to your feet and a light to your path**, how will you know where to go if you do not know the Word?
- **If God watches over His Word to perform it**, how will you know what God will, can, and wants to do if you do not know the Word?

When God's Words Are Proven TRUE, Faith Soars!

Can you recall the time when John the Baptist had a moment of doubt and sent two of his disciples to Jesus to verify if He was the Christ?

Luke 7:22-23
> And He (Jesus) answered them, "Go and tell John what you have **seen** and **heard**: the blind receive their sight, the lame walk, lepers are cleansed, and the deaf hear, the dead are raised up, the poor have good news to them. And blessed be the one who is not offended by Me."

Why did He answer John like this? It's because that was exactly what the prophets and the Scriptures had said about the coming anointed one, the Christ, the Messiah!

Isn't it awesome?! But for John the Baptist to have believed and known that Jesus was the "one who was to come", he had to have known what the Scriptures had said about the Messiah or he wouldn't have understood Jesus' answer! Boom!

When God's words are proven true, and people see, touch, and experience the signs and wonders that God promised, faith soars higher and higher!

Glory to Glory Q&A

Describe the times in your life (if any) when you felt that God had failed you. For each incident that comes to mind, please answer the following:

1. Describe the incident.
2. What was your reaction?
   Were you hurt? Did you stop reading your Bible? Were you afraid to trust God again?
3. Were there other people involved in this incident? If so, did you/can you forgive them, pray for them, and bless them?
4. How do you honestly, in your heart of hearts, feel about these people and about God?
5. How are these feelings helping you and serving you?
6. Will you be willing to give this whole incident and every hurt and feeling that goes with it to Jesus and ask Him to heal you in return?
   If so, then just imagine putting the whole incident, everything and everyone together, in one big bundle and handing everything over to Jesus.

God Led Israel Out of Egypt and Into the Promised Land

Abraham had a son, Isaac, who had a son, Jacob, whose name was changed to Israel.

Why Did God Choose Israel as His People?

God's passion for Israel is a demonstration and a reassurance of what God would do for those He loves, so they may know Him and accept Him as their Savior, Redeemer, and the one who wants to fight on their behalf.

There is **faith**… and then there is to **know**... to be absolutely certain beyond a shadow of a doubt.

God didn't want anyone to ever again have any doubts that He alone is the one and only true, living God!

He wanted everyone to be able to trust Him and have faith in Him. He is the Beloved Faith Maker.

He still performs mighty miracles for those who believe and trust in Him.

What about the Gentiles?

If God wanted to show the world what He would do for the ones He loves, don't you think that God also wanted to show the world what would happen to people who did not have a living God who fought for them...?

Always keep in mind that everything happened for a reason. God is not confused. The Word says that Christ came at the appointed time.

Father God's plan was to reconcile both Jews and Gentiles, through Christ, into one household and be the Father of them all (Ephesians 2), fulfilling His promise to Abraham.

The nations of old had paid the price for us to have a Bible, packed with testimonies, that we may obtain faith and prosper.

Signs Were Given That All May Believe and Know That He Is God

You know the history that the descendants of Jacob (called Israel) became slaves in Egypt because the Egyptians had appointed a new king who did not know Joseph.

Joseph was a ruler in Egypt by God's will, as He worked everything that happened in Joseph's life together for good (Genesis 50:20). God positioned Joseph in Egypt, so that he could provide for God's people during a time of famine. Israel were many people and the Pharaoh was afraid of them and started to oppress them.

When the people cried out to God, He heard them, and remembered His covenant with Abraham, Isaac, and Jacob.

Already there was a man named Moses, whom God had predestined for this task of leading His people out of Egypt and into Canaan, the land that God had promised Abraham. At the time, Israel was to literally be heirs of the land Canaan and physically take possession of it as the Promised Land. The Lord gave Moses signs and wonders to perform so that the Hebrews would know that God had sent Moses and believe.

In Exodus 4:4-5, after turning Moses' staff into a snake, the Lord said to him:

> "Put out your hand and catch it by the tail" – so he put out his hand and caught it, and it became a staff in his hand – "that they may **believe** that the Lord, the God of their fathers, the God of Abraham, the God of Isaac, and the God of Jacob, has appeared to you."

God raised up Pharaoh and hardened his heart. God sent the plagues to show His power and that who He was, and what He was able to do, were shown publicly for the entire world to see. This was done so that all may **know** that there is none like God in all the earth, and that they may **know** that the earth is the Lord's (Exodus 8:10, Romans 9:17)!

Exodus 9:16, and 10:2
> "But for this purpose I have raised you up, to show you My power, so that My name may be proclaimed in all the earth.
>
> ... and that you may tell in the hearing of your son and of your grandson how I have dealt harshly with the Egyptians and what signs I have done among them, that you may know that I am the LORD."

God's Covenant with Israel, and God's Warning

In Exodus 19:4-6, you find the covenant that God made with His beloved Israel saying:

> "You yourselves have seen what I did to the Egyptians, and how I bore you on eagle's wings and brought you to Myself. Now therefore, if you will indeed obey My voice and keep My covenant, you shall be **My treasured possession** among all peoples, for all the earth is Mine; and you shall be to Me a kingdom of priests and a holy nation."

Exodus 34:10&12-17
> And He said, "Behold, I am making a **covenant**. Before all your people I will do marvels, such as have not been created in all the earth or in any nation. And all the people among whom you are shall see the work of the Lord, for it is an awesome thing that I will do with you.
>
> Take care, lest you make a covenant with the inhabitants of the land to which you go, lest it becomes a snare in your midst. You shall tear down their altars and break their pillars and cut down their Asherim (for you shall worship no other god, for the Lord, whose name is Jealous, is a jealous God), lest you make a covenant with the inhabitants of the land, and when they whore after their gods and sacrifice to their gods and you are invited, you eat of his sacrifice, and you take of their daughters for your sons, and their daughters whore after their gods and make your sons whore after their gods. You shall not make yourselves any gods of cast metal."

Exodus 19:9
> And the Lord said to Moses, "Behold, I am coming to you in a thick cloud, that the people may **hear** when I speak with you, and may also **believe** you forever."

God's GLORY

There are three ways in which God reveals His glory:

1) His manifest presence, as He appeared in the thick cloud that the people could sense, see, and hear Him and believe (Exodus 19,34)
2) His ability and power, by the signs and wonders He performed (John 2:11, John 11:40-44)
3) His character (Exodus 33:18-19 & 34:6-7)

When Moses wanted to see God's glory (Exodus 34:6-7), the Lord passed before him and proclaimed, "The Lord, the Lord, a God merciful and gracious, slow to anger, and abounding in steadfast love and faithfulness, keeping steadfast love for thousands, forgiving iniquity and transgression and sin, but who will by no means clear the guilty, visiting the iniquity of the fathers on the children and the children's children, to the third and the fourth generation."

(Keep in mind that at the appointed time, God mercifully sent His Son to take the punishment for sin - 2 Corinthians 5:17-21, Isaiah 53:4-5,10)

God's glory is not just about falling over and experiencing the power of God. It is also healing and wonders, and it is also God's character.

God's glory isn't meant to be experienced only on the outside, but also in the hearts and minds of people.

God Wanted to Live Amongst His People, to Be With Them, Lead Them, and Love Them

God gave Moses the template of the tabernacle to be built, so that God could live amongst His people – a desire that God had since creation – to live with man! He gave explicit instructions for the layout and construction of the tabernacle, and the consecration of all the utensils and everything that was part of the tabernacle, so that God could be in their midst, without anybody getting hurt because of Him.

For He said that no man may see God and live, because of their sins. The instruction to enter His presence only when justified by the blood of animals and the oil was meant for their protection and not for their harm. After the cross, by the blood of Christ that was shed as an offering for sin, we are now able to enter the spiritual Holy of Holies, the throne room of God (Hebrews 10:10,12-14, 17-18, 19-23).

Under the New Covenant, Jesus Christ, the Lamb of God came to make atonement for the sins of the world, reconciling man to God.

Under the Old Covenant, atonement for sins was made by the offering of the blood of animals.

Circumcised Hearts

What happened to some people in Israel was that they performed the cleansing rituals as habit, or duty, but not from the heart.

Jesus said that those were cleaning the outside of the cup, without cleaning the inside.

It was always God's intention that His people would serve Him with all of their hearts, and that when they made mistakes, they would come to Him with a circumcised heart. This meant that they had real repentance and remorse of their wrongdoing. He never intended for them to only perform rituals without love towards Him.

The Lord hates pride but gives grace and mercy to the humble – to those with a circumcised heart.

Leviticus 26:40-42 (ISV)
> "Nevertheless, when they confess their iniquity, the iniquity of their ancestors, and their unfaithfulness by which they acted unfaithfully against Me by living life contrary to Me, causing Me to oppose them and take them to the land of their enemies so that the uncircumcised foreskin of their hearts can be humbled and so that they accept the punishment of their iniquity, then I'll remember My covenant with Jacob, My covenant with Isaac, and My covenant with Abraham. I'll also remember the land."

The Lord's Blessing

The Lord told Moses to teach Aaron and his sons to bless His people by declaring over them:

Numbers 6:24-27
> "The Lord bless you and keep you; the Lord make His face shine upon you and be gracious to you; the Lord lift up His countenance upon you and give you peace. So shall they put My Name upon the people of Israel, and I will bless them."

God took pleasure in giving Israel His name, His everything. All the people of the earth knew that Israel were the Lord's people.

God's name is the heart and soul of God. It is who He is.

The Lord's Glory by His Presence Being With Them and Leading Them

God's glory accompanied Israel as they travelled through the desert.

Numbers 9:15-18 (ISV)
> On the same morning that the tent was set up, a cloud covered the tent, that is, the Tent of Testimony, and in the evening fire appeared over the tent until morning.
>
> It was so continuously - there was a cloud covering by day, and a fire cloud appeared at night.
>
> Whenever the cloud above the tent ascended, the Israelis would travel and encamp in the place where the cloud settled.
>
> According to whatever the LORD said, the Israelis would travel. According to whatever the LORD said, they would camp as long as the cloud remained over the Tent of Meeting.

Blow the Trumpet!

Growing up, music and singing were a great part of our lives at home and at school, because my mother was a music teacher. As long as I can remember, my mother had music students in our home to teach. At some point, she was also involved with the cadets and I can still recall the sounds of trumpets and other blowing instruments as they were practicing for competitions.

Then I read that the Lord gave Israel instruction to make two silver trumpets (Numbers 10:1-10). They were to blow the trumpets in different ways for different types of assemblies and occasions. What I just love about this was that the Lord said, "The blowing of the trumpet shall be a reminder of you before your God: I am the Lord your God."

When going to war, when travelling, when gathering and assembling together, when rejoicing, or making burnt offerings, peace offerings, or on the day of gladness – they were to blow the trumpet!

For the Lord your God is with you, whatever you are going through!

Blow the trumpet!

Israel's Unbelief and the Lord's Sorrow

After sending the spies to Canaan, and having them return with only Caleb and Joshua having faith while the rest of the spies were shivering with fear and rebelling in unbelief, the Lord said to Moses, "How long will this people despise Me? And how long will they not believe in Me, in spite of all the signs that I have done among them? (Numbers 14:11)"

Moses interceded for the people, and the Lord pardoned them, but their unbelief had dire consequences, except for Caleb and Joshua for they followed the Lord fully.

Numbers 14:20-24
> Then the LORD said, "I have pardoned, according to your word.
>
> But truly, as I live, and as all the earth shall be filled with the glory of the LORD, none of the men who have seen My glory and My signs that I did in Egypt and in the wilderness, and yet have put Me to the test these ten times and have not obeyed My voice, shall see the land that I swore to give to their fathers. And none of those who despised Me shall see it.
>
> But My servant Caleb, because he has a different spirit and has followed Me fully, I will bring into the land into which he went, and his descendants shall possess it.

Those Who Rejected the Lord, Didn't Enter the Promised Land

Numbers 14:28-33
> Say to them, 'As I live, declares the Lord, what you have said in My hearing I will do to you: your dead bodies shall fall in this wilderness, and all of your number, listed in the census from twenty years old and upward, who have grumbled against Me, not one shall come into the land where I swore that I would make you dwell, except Caleb the son of Jephunneh and Joshua the son of Nun. But your little ones, who you said would become a prey, I will bring in, and they shall know the land that you have rejected. But as for you, your dead bodies shall fall in this wilderness. And your children shall be shepherds in the wilderness forty years and shall suffer for your faithlessness, until the last of your dead bodies lies in the wilderness.

So now you know. Those Israelites perished in the wilderness – not because God was mean, but because of their unbelief and rejection of the Lord's love and care.

Even Moses lost the plot and didn't enter Canaan because of his disrespect and unbelief at Meribah: The assembly of people was complaining that there was no water to drink and they were angry at Moses for leading them out of Egypt (Numbers 20:2-12).

Moses and Aaron went to the entrance of the tent of meeting and fell on their faces. The glory of the LORD appeared to them, and the Lord said to Moses (Numbers 20:8), "Take the staff and assemble the congregation, you and Aaron your brother, and **tell** the rock before their eyes to yield its water. So you shall bring water out of the rock for them and give drink to the congregation and to their cattle."

Numbers 20:10-12
> Then Moses and Aaron gathered the assembly together before the rock, and he said to them, "<u>Hear now, you rebels</u>: shall we bring water for you out of this rock?" And Moses lifted up his hand and <u>struck the rock with his staff twice</u>, and water came out abundantly, and the congregation drank and their livestock.
>
> And the Lord said to Moses and Aaron, "<u>Because you did not believe in Me</u>, to uphold Me as holy in the eyes of the people of Israel, therefore you shall not bring this assembly into the land that I have given them."

God gave Moses an instruction to **tell** the rock before the eyes of the people to yield its water. When God gives an instruction, He always has a very good reason why He gives the instruction.

What I believe the Lord was actually saying, when He was telling Moses that he didn't believe Him when he struck the rock instead of talking to it, is, "There was something that would have happened in the hearts of the people when all you had to do was to speak to the rock for the water to come out. You didn't trust me, Moses, to know what I asked you to do. When I say things, I have a reason for saying them."

Jesus, the Messiah, Prophesied in the Wilderness

When the people became impatient and were complaining again about food and water, the Lord sent fiery serpents among them and they bit them.

Then the Lord said to Moses, "Make a fiery serpent and set it on a pole, and everyone who is bitten, when he sees it, shall live." So Moses made a bronze serpent and set it on a pole. And if a serpent bit anyone, he would look at the bronze serpent and live. (Numbers 21:4-9)

When Jesus proclaimed in John 12:32, "And I, when I am lifted up from the earth, will draw all people to myself", this scripture was fulfilled.

Israel Betrayed God's Love, by Whoring after Other Gods

While Israel lived in Shittim, the people began to whore with the daughters of Moab. These invited the people to the sacrifices of their gods, and the people ate and bowed down to their gods. So Israel yoked them to Baal of Peor.

The anger of the Lord was kindled against Israel. Phinehas acted on behalf of the Lord and the Lord commended his actions by saying that He gives Phinehas and his descendants a covenant of peace, because he was jealous for his God and made atonement for the people of Israel (Numbers 25:1-13).

God values people who intercede on behalf of His people, like Phinehas did here.

Many times, Israel would "file for divorce" from the Lord, rejecting Him and running after other powerless gods.

Moses' Last Instructions to the People of Israel

Before Moses' death, as Israel was about to enter the Promised Land under Joshua's leadership, Moses spoke to the people, remembering the Lord's steadfast love and care over the past 40 years.

1. The Lord's Promise to Fight for Them, and Their Unbelief

Moses recalled the people being afraid of the Amorites because they were greater and taller than them and their cities were big.

Deuteronomy 1:29-32
> Then I (Moses) said to you, "Do not be in dread or afraid of them. The Lord your God who goes before you will Himself fight for you, just as He did for you in Egypt before your eyes, and in the wilderness, where you have seen how the Lord your God carried you, as a man carries his son, all the way that you went until you came to this place." Yet in spite of this word, you did not believe the Lord your God."

2. That You May Know the Lord is God, There Is No Other

In Deuteronomy 4:33-35 & 39 Moses continued saying:

> "Did any people ever hear the voice of a god speaking out of the midst of the fire, as you have heard, and still live? Or has any god ever attempted to go and take a nation for himself from the midst of another nation, by trials, by signs, by wonders, and by war, by a mighty hand and an outstretched arm, and by great deeds of terror, all of which the LORD your God did for you in Egypt before your eyes?

> To you it was shown, that you might **know** that the Lord is God; there is no other besides Him.

> **Know** therefore today, and lay it in your heart, that the Lord is God in heaven above and on the earth beneath; there is no other."

3. Moses' Earnest Warning to Israel to Teach Their Children

Deuteronomy 6:4-9
> "Hear, O Israel: The Lord our God, the Lord is one. You shall love the Lord your God with all your heart and with all your soul and with all your might. And these words that I command you today shall be on your

heart. You shall <u>teach them diligently to your children</u>, and shall <u>talk</u> of them when you <u>sit</u> in your house, and when you <u>walk</u> by the way, and when you <u>lie</u> down, and when you <u>rise</u>. You shall bind them as a sign on your hand, and they shall be as frontlets between your eyes. You shall write them on the doorposts of your house and on your gates."

Years later, David wrote in Psalms 16:8, "I have the Lord always before me; because He is at my right hand I shall not be shaken!" This was also quoted by the Apostle Peter in his sermon at Pentecost as recorded by Luke in Acts 2:25.

4. Man Lives by Every Word That Comes From the Mouth of God

Deuteronomy 8:2-3
> And you shall remember the whole way that the Lord your God has led you these forty years in the wilderness, that He might humble you, testing you to know what is in your heart, whether you would keep His commandments or not.
>
> And He humbled you and let you hunger and fed you with manna, which you did not know, nor did your fathers know, that He might make you know that man does not live by bread alone, but man lives by every word that comes from the mouth of the Lord.

When satan tempted Jesus when He was hungry, this was the scripture that Jesus used to rebuke him (Matthew 4:4) because He knew the truth of this scripture and couldn't be tempted by fleshly desires.

5. It Is the LORD Who Provides for You and Gives You Victory, Because He Promised He Would

Deuteronomy 8:16-18
> Who fed you in the wilderness with manna that your fathers did not know, that He might humble you and test you, to do you good in the end. Beware lest you say in your heart, "My power and the might of my hand have gotten me this wealth."
>
> You shall remember the Lord your God, for it is He who gives you power to get wealth that He may confirm His covenant that He swore to your fathers, as it is this day.

Deuteronomy 9:3
> **Know** therefore today that He who goes over before you as a consuming fire is the Lord your God. He will destroy them (your enemies) and subdue them before you. So you shall drive them out and make them perish quickly, as the Lord has promised you.

Deuteronomy 9:5-6
> Not because of your righteousness or the uprightness of your heart are you going in to possess their land, but because of the wickedness of these nations the Lord your God is driving them out from before you, and that He may confirm the word that the Lord swore to your fathers, to Abraham, to Isaac, and to Jacob. Know therefore, that the Lord your God is not giving you this good land to possess because of your righteousness, for you are a stubborn people.

6. What Does the Lord Require of You?

Deuteronomy 10:12&16
> And now, Israel, what does the Lord your God require of you, but to <u>fear</u> the Lord your God, to <u>walk</u> in all His ways, to <u>love</u> Him, to <u>serve</u> the Lord your God with <u>all your heart and with all your soul.</u>
>
> Circumcise therefore the foreskin of your heart, and <u>be no longer stubborn</u>.

Deuteronomy 11:16-18(KJV)
> Take heed to yourselves, that your heart be not deceived, and ye turn aside, and serve other gods, and worship them;
>
> And then the LORD'S wrath be kindled against you, and He shut up the heaven, that there be no rain, and that the land yield not her fruit; and lest ye perish quickly from off the good land which the LORD giveth you.
>
> Therefore shall ye lay up these my words in your heart and in your soul, and bind them for a sign upon your hand, that they may be as frontlets between your eyes.

7. The Lord's Blessing

Deuteronomy 14:2 (ISV)
> Because you are a holy people to the LORD your God, and the LORD chose to make you His precious possession from among all the peoples of the earth.

Deuteronomy 15:6 (ISV)
> Because the LORD your God will bless you just as He promised. You are to lend to many nations, but not borrow. Also, you will rule over many nations, but they will not rule over you.

Deuteronomy 20:1&4 (ISV)
> When you go to war against your enemies and observe more horses, chariots, and soldiers than you have, don't be afraid of them, for the LORD your God who brought you out of the land of Egypt is with you.

For the LORD your God will be with you, fighting on your behalf against your enemies in order to grant you victory.

Deuteronomy 28:8 (ISV)
> The LORD will send blessings for you with regard to your barns and everything you undertake. Indeed, He will bless you in the land that the LORD your God is about to give you.

Deuteronomy 29:5-6 (ISV)
> "Though I've led you for 40 years in the desert, neither your clothes nor your shoes have worn out. You didn't have bread to eat or wine or anything intoxicating to drink, so that you would learn that I am the LORD your God."

Deuteronomy 29:9 (ISV)
> Therefore, keep the terms of this covenant, carrying them out so that you'll be wise in everything you do.

8. Warning about the Root of Bitterness

Deuteronomy 29:18-20 (ISV)
> Be alert so there is no man, woman, family, or a tribe whose heart is turning away from the LORD your God to go and serve the gods of those nations. Be alert so there will be no root among you that produces poisonous and bitter fruit, because when such a person hears the words of this oath, he will bless himself and say:
>
> 'I will have a peaceful life, even though I'm determined to be stubborn.' By doing this he will be sweeping away both watered and parched ground alike.'
>
> The LORD won't forgive such a person. Instead, the zealous anger of the LORD will blaze against him. All the curses that were written in this book will fall on him. Then the LORD will wipe out his memory from under heaven.

The writer of the book of Hebrews also warns in Hebrews 12:15: "See to it that no one fails to obtain the grace of God; that no "root of bitterness" springs up and causes trouble, and by it many become defiled."

Bitterness is a result of unforgiveness, pride, stubbornness, resentment, suppressed anger, and hurt. A hardened heart that is filled with bitterness, has difficulty to love, hope, and believe. Even though the love of God has been poured out into our hearts by the Holy Spirit that's been given by God, a wall of bitterness and resentment not only locks up the hurt and builds a wall to keep hurt out, but it also locks up the love from pouring out.

9. Punishment by Jewish Law for Crime unto Death – to Hang on a Tree – Jesus' Death Foretold

Deuteronomy 21:22-23 (ISV)
> "If a man is guilty of a capital offense, is executed, and then is impaled on a tree, his body must not remain overnight on the tree. You must bury him that same day, because cursed of God is the one who has been hanged on a tree. Don't defile your land that the LORD is about to give you as your inheritance."

Paul wrote in Galatians 3:13-14: "Christ redeemed us from the curse of the law by becoming a curse for us – for it is written, "Cursed is everyone who is hanged on a tree"– so that in Christ Jesus the blessing of Abraham might come to the Gentiles, so that we might receive the promised Spirit through faith.

Joshua Leads the People into Canaan and Divides the Land

God reassured Joshua of His promises and He repeated His warning for them to obey His law.

Joshua 1:3, 5&7 (ISV)
> "I'm giving you every place where the sole of your foot falls, just as I promised Moses.
>
> No one will be victorious against you for the rest of your life. I'll be with you just like I was with Moses – I'll neither fail you nor abandon you.
>
> Only be strong and very courageous to ensure that you obey all the instructions that My servant Moses gave you – turn neither to the right nor to the left from it – so that you may succeed wherever you go."

Rahab's Faith

As you know, Rahab was a prostitute and a Gentile who lived in Jericho, the first town in Canaan, the Promised Land that Israel took possession of.

And because of her faith in God, she and her family were saved.

Furthermore, she didn't remain a prostitute, for the Lord transformed her life and blessed her to be part of the genealogy of Jesus Christ! She married Salmon, and they became the parents of Boaz. That made her the mother-in-law of Ruth, and the great-great-grandmother of David!

God is moved by faith, keeping His promise to Abraham.

Following is Rahab's declaration of faith to the spies who stayed in her house.

Joshua 2:9-11
"I **know** that the Lord has given you the land, and that the fear of you has fallen upon us, and that all the inhabitants of the land melt away before you. For we have **heard** how the Lord dried up the water of the Red Sea before you when you came out of Egypt, and what you did to the two kings of the Amorites who were beyond the Jordan, to Sihon and Og, whom you devoted to destruction.

And as soon as we heard it, our hearts melted, and there was no spirit left in any man because of you, for the LORD your God, He is God in the heavens above and on the earth beneath."

Another Mighty Work of God as He Dried up the Waters of the Jordan – That They May KNOW!

Joshua 4:23-24
For the Lord your God dried up the waters of the river Jordan for you until you passed over, as the Lord your God did to the Red Sea, which he dried up for us until we passed over, so that all the peoples of the earth may **know** that the hand of the Lord is mighty, that you may *fear the Lord your God forever.

*Meaning respect and honor

ALL the Promises of God Came to Pass

Just one last reminder before moving on to the Judges.

Joshua21:45
"Not one word of all the good promises that the Lord had made to the house of Israel had failed; all came to pass."

Glory to Glory Q&A

1. When looking at Caleb's faith, what feelings are stirred up in you? (Referring to Numbers 13, Numbers 14:1-38 and Joshua 14:6-15)
2. How does it make you feel knowing that God fulfilled every promise that He had made to Israel to lead them into the Promised Land?
3. Think about events in your own life over the past month. How has God helped you?

Chapter 4

The Period When the Judges Led God's People

The names of the Judges: Othnil, Ehud, Shamgar, Deborah (and Barak), Gideon, Tola, Jair, Jephthah, Ibzan, Elon, Abdon, Samson, Eli and Samuel.

Why Did God Appoint Judges?

After Joshua's death, and the passing of all of that generation, there arose another generation after them who did not know the Lord or the work that He had done in Israel (Judges 2:10).

Remember that the Lord had told them to teach their children? Well, they didn't, but because of God's steadfast love and mercy, He appointed judges to lead His people and encourage them to have faith in Him.

Israel Whored After Other Gods

Then people of Israel did what was evil in the sight of the Lord by abandoning the Lord and they started serving the Baals. They went after other gods, from among the gods of the people who were around them and bowed down to them. They provoked the Lord to anger.

He gave them over to plunderers who plundered them, and He sold them into the hand of their surrounding enemies, so that they could no longer withstand their enemies.

Whenever they marched out, the hand of the Lord was against them for harm, as the Lord had warned, and as the Lord had sworn to them. They were in terrible distress.

Then the Lord raised up judges, who saved them out of the hand of those who plundered them. Yet they did not listen to their judges, for they whored after other gods and bowed down to them. They soon turned away from the way that their fathers walked, who had obeyed the commandments of the Lord, but they did not do so (Judges 2:11-17).

The Lord Pitied, Saved, Then Tested Them

Judges 2:18-22 (ISV)
> "As a result, whenever the LORD raised up leaders for them, the LORD remained present with their leader, delivering Israel from the control of their enemies during the lifetime of that leader. The LORD was moved with compassion by their groaning that had been caused by those who were oppressing and persecuting them.
>
> However, after the leader had died, they would relapse to a condition more corrupt than their ancestors, following other gods, serving them, and worshipping them. They would not abandon their activities or their obstinate lifestyles.
>
> In His burning anger against Israel, the LORD said, "Because the people have transgressed My covenant that I commanded their ancestors to keep, and because they haven't obeyed Me,
>
> I'm also going to stop expelling any of the nations that remained after Joshua died.
>
> That way, I'll use them to demonstrate (test) whether or not Israel will keep the LORD's lifestyle by walking on that road like their ancestors did."

The Lord's Heart Remained Steadfast

Judges chapter 7 tells the incident of Gideon's 300 men. Read how beautiful this is. Judges 7:2&7:

> Then Lord said to Gideon, "The people with you are too many for Me to give the Midianites into their hand, lest Israel boast over Me saying, 'My own hand has saved me.'

And the Lord said to Gideon, "With the 300 men who lapped I will save you and give the Midianites into your hand, and let all the others go every man to his home."

Isn't the Lord just amazing? He wants to be your Savior and fight for you!

He wants to be your hero. If you should look at your own circumstances thinking, "Only God can fix this mess..." it sounds like a task that God would be interested in...

Judges 8:22-23 (paraphrased):

Then (can you believe this), the men of Israel said to Gideon, "Rule over us, you and your son and your grandson, because you saved us from the Midianites."

(Fortunately) Gideon said to them, "I will not rule over you, and my son will not rule over you; the Lord will rule over you!"

Grace for Ruth Also

Ruth, a Moabite and a Gentile, also found grace with the Lord because she faithfully pledged her loyalty to the God of Naomi.

Ruth 1:16-17:
> But Ruth said, "Do not urge me to leave you or to return from following you. For where you go I will go, and where you lodge I will lodge. Your people shall be my people, and your God my God. Where you die I will die, and there will I be buried. May the LORD do so to me and more also if anything but death part me from you."

Ruth obeyed the instructions that the Lord gave to her through Naomi, and Boaz became her redeemer. Thereby, she became David's grandmother and part of the genealogy of Jesus Christ!

Samuel (1060 – 1020 BC)

Samuel was the last of the judges of Israel.

God raised him in the house of the priest Eli, who taught Samuel to know the voice of the Lord. The Lord appointed Samuel a prophet in Israel and he obeyed the voice of the Lord diligently.

1 Samuel 3:19:
> And Samuel grew, and the LORD was with him and let none of his words fall to the ground.

He judged all the days of his life and then his two sons became judges, but they did not walk in his ways and took bribes and turned aside after gain.

Then all the elders gathered, and Israel demanded to have a king to govern them.

 Glory to Glory Q&A

1. Why do you think God instructed Israel to teach their children to follow Him?
2. Take a look at 1 Samuel 3 where Samuel was already serving the Lord in the presence of Eli. When God called his name, he didn't recognize God's voice.
   Can you hear the voice of God? If so, how does He speak to you and how often do you listen to Him?

Israel's First Three Kings

The Earthly Kings, Demanded by the People

Israel said that they wanted a king so that they could *"be like all the other nations in that their king would judge them, and go out before them and fight their battles"* (1 Samuel 8:20).

Do you hear this..?! Israel, the Lord's beloved, His treasured possession, rejected Him, their Almighty God who had been fighting for them all along, as their King!

After the people demanded a king, Samuel prayed to the Lord.

Samuel 8:7
> And the Lord said to Samuel, "Obey the voice of the people in all that they say to you, for they have not rejected you, but they have rejected Me from being king over them."

The Lord was deeply grieved about the rejection of Israel, and gave Samuel the following word:

1 Samuel 10:18-19
> And he said to the people of Israel, "Thus says the LORD, the God of Israel, 'I brought up Israel out of Egypt, and I delivered you from the hand of the Egyptians and from the hand of all the kingdoms that were

oppressing you.' But today you have rejected your God, who saves you from all your calamities and your distresses, and you have said to Him, 'Set a king over us.'

The Lord Anointed Saul to Be King (1051 – 1011 BC)

God told Samuel to earnestly warn the people and show them the ways of kingship – that the king will reign over them and that they will have to obey and serve him (1 Samuel 8:11-19), but still the people demanded a king.

Then the Lord revealed to Samuel who to anoint as king, and he anointed Saul as the first king (in the flesh) of Israel, to reign over them and to save them from their enemies. He took a flask of oil and poured it out on Saul's head and kissed him (1 Samuel 10:1).

The Lord gave him signs to confirm that He has anointed Saul to be prince over His people. One of the signs was that, *"the Spirit of the Lord will rush upon you, and you will prophesy with them and be turned into another man."* (1 Samuel 10:6)

Samuel Cautioned the People to Obey and Serve the Lord with All Their Heart

In Samuel's farewell address, he reminded the people that the Lord will not forsake His people, and that they needed to take care to obey His voice and not to go after empty things (1 Samuel 12).

He earnestly warned them to follow God with all their heart, and to always remember the great things He had done for them.

Saul's Breach of Faith and His Disobedience

Saul acted independently and offered an unlawful sacrifice to keep the people with him, instead of seeking the Lord's favor and doing what He said (1 Samuel 13:8-13).

1 Samuel 13:14 (Samuel speaks to Saul):
"But now your kingdom shall not continue. The Lord has sought out a man after His own heart and the Lord has commanded him to be prince over His people, because you have not kept what the Lord commanded you."

And Samuel said, "Has the Lord as great delight in burnt offerings and sacrifices, as in obeying His voice? To **obey** is better than sacrifice, and to **listen** than the fat of rams. For rebellion is as the sin of witchcraft and divination, and stubbornness is as wickedness and idolatry. Because you have rejected the word of the Lord, He has also rejected you from being king" (1 Samuel 15:22-24).

Saul said to Samuel, "I have sinned, for I have transgressed the commandment of the Lord and your words, <u>because I was afraid of the people and obeyed their voice</u>."

Years later, Saul died <u>for his breach of faith</u>. He broke faith with the Lord in that he did not do what the Lord instructed him to do, and he also consulted a medium for guidance instead of praying to God and asking Him (1Chronicles 10:13).

Why Was David Chosen by God to be Anointed as King?

God called David *"a man after His own heart, <u>for he will obey and do all My will.</u>"* (Acts 13:22)

The Lord was deeply touched by David's love for Him and He made an everlasting covenant with David.

Following are 10 very endearing qualities that separated David from all other future kings of Israel and Judah.

1. The Lord Saw David's Heart

The Lord had sent Samuel to Jesse's house to anoint David, but Jesse's other sons were presented to him first.

But the Lord said to Samuel, "Do not look on Eliab's (one of Jesse's sons) appearance or on how tall he is, because I have rejected him. For the Lord sees not as man sees: man looks on outward appearance, but the Lord looks on the heart" (1 Samuel 16:7).

1 Samuel 16:11-13

> Then Samuel said to Jesse, "Are all your sons here?" And he said, "There remains yet the youngest, but behold, he is keeping the sheep."
>
> And Samuel said to Jesse, "Send and get him, for we will not sit down till he comes here."
>
> And he sent and brought him in. Now he was ruddy and had beautiful eyes and was handsome. And the LORD said, "Arise, anoint him, for this is he."
>
> Then Samuel took the horn of oil and anointed him in the midst of his brothers. And the Spirit of the LORD rushed upon David from that day forward.

2. The Lord Knew That David Had Relentless Faith in Him!

Nobody wanted to face Goliath, and everyone who heard him and saw him was too afraid of him.

When David went to take food for his brothers, he heard the chants and insults of Goliath.

Then David asked the men who stood by him about the *"uncircumcised Philistine who dares defy the armies of the living God!"*

He then volunteered to face Goliath for he believed that, *"The Lord who delivered me from the paw of the lion and from the paw of the bear will deliver me from the hand of this Philistine."* (1 Samuel 17:37)

1 Samuel 17:45-47
> Then David said to the Philistine, "You come to me with a sword and a spear and a javelin, but I come to you in the name of the Lord of hosts, the God of the armies of Israel, whom you have defied.
>
> This day the Lord will deliver you into my hand, and I will strike you down and cut off your head. And I will give the dead bodies of the host of the Philistines this day to the birds of the air and to the wild beasts of the earth, that all the earth may **know** that there is a God in Israel, and that all this assembly may **know** that the Lord saves not with sword and spear. For the battle is the Lord's, and He will give you into my hand."

So, David had five pebbles, his slingshot, and his faith in the Lord. The Philistine was struck down dead with the first strike of the first pebble. I can just imagine the Lord saying to David, "The five pebbles were too many, David, for it was your faith in Me that made all the difference!"

3. David Was Commander of the Broken

David served Saul, and Saul tried to kill David, so he had to flee from Saul's attacks.

At some point, David found refuge in the cave of Adullam. When his brothers and everyone in his father's house heard it, they went down there to him.

About 400 men who were troubled, in debt, or had bitterness, came to him and he became their leader and commander (1 Samuel 22:1-2).

4. David Honored God's Anointed

More than once, David could have killed Saul, but refused to do it for he honored God's anointed (1 Samuel 26:9).

5. David Strengthened Himself in the Lord

When the Philistines rejected David, and his wives were captured, David was greatly distressed, for the people spoke of stoning him, because all the people were very bitter. David's reaction was to <u>strengthen himself in the Lord his God</u> (1 Samuel 30:6).

The psalms of David are like reading his daily journal that he kept with the Lord.

He was always having conversations with God - praising the Lord, crying out and being real and honest with Him, and receiving words from the Lord, as he found his strength and comfort in Him.

6. David Knew He Was King to Benefit God's People

One thing that becomes very clear in the Old Testament is how much God values leaders who look after His people and protect and lead them to follow in His ways and values.

2 Samuel 5:12 (ISV)
> So David concluded that the LORD had established him as king over Israel and that he had exalted his kingdom in order to benefit his people Israel. (Also 1 Chronicles 14:2, 1 Chronicles 18:14)

David knew the responsibility of leading God's people. He knew that God made him king, and that he was made king not to exalt himself, but that he may lead God's people in a way that they may know and follow Him with all of their heart.

7. David's Humble and Teachable Character as Revealed by the Incident with the Ark

1 Chronicles 13 (paraphrased):

David consulted with the commanders of thousands, and of hundreds and with every leader saying, "If it seems good to you and from the Lord our God, let us bring the ark of our God to us, as we did not do in the days of Saul." All the assembly agreed to do so, for the thing was right in the eyes of all the people.

So David assembled all Israel to bring the ark of God from Kiriath-jearim, to Jerusalem.

And David and Israel were celebrating wholeheartedly before God, singing songs and playing on lyres, harps, tambourines, cymbals and trumpets.

When they came to the threshing floor of Chidon, the oxen stumbled, and Uzzah put out his hand to keep the ark from falling. Then the anger of the

LORD rose against Uzzah, and He struck him down because he put out his hand to the ark, and he died.

David's Reaction to Uzzah's Death

And David was <u>angry</u> because the LORD had broken out against Uzzah.

And David was <u>afraid</u> of God that day, and he said, "<u>How can I bring the ark of God home to me?</u>"

David stopped and took the ark aside to the house of Obed-edom, where the ark stayed for three months. While the ark stayed there, the Lord blessed Obed-edom's household and everything that he had. So David did not take the ark home into the city of David, but took it aside.

When they were ready to bring the ark back the second time, David said to those gathered together to carry the ark, in 1 Chronicles 15:12-15 (paraphrased):

"You are the heads of the fathers' houses of the Levites. Consecrate yourselves, you and your brothers, so that you may bring up the ark of the LORD, the God of Israel, to the place that I have prepared for it. Because you did not carry it the first time, the LORD our God broke out against us, <u>because we did not seek Him according to the rule</u>."

So, the priests and the Levites consecrated themselves and carried the ark of God on their shoulders with the poles, as Moses had commanded according to the word of the LORD.

David also commanded the chiefs of the Levites to appoint the singers, and the appointed musicians to play loudly on instruments, harps, lyres and cymbals, to raise sounds of joy!

David's reaction to Uzzah's death was first anger, and then he feared the Lord and realized that he didn't consult the Lord about the matter. Then he repented and sought and followed the Lord's instruction in how to bring the ark back!

No wonder that the Lord wanted David to be leader of His people. For he sought to do things God's way, and even when he made a mistake, he took ownership and fixed it, God's way.

8. David Established Worship and Prophesied Using Instruments

David appointed worshippers to offer thanksgiving and praises to the Lord in the temple, with instruments that he had made (1 Chronicles 23:2-5, 26-31).

1 Chronicles 25:1

David and the chiefs of the service also set apart for the service the sons of Asaph, and of Heman, and of Jeduthun, who <u>prophesied</u> with lyres, with harps, and with cymbals.

9. David Trained His People to Flow in the Anointing and to Excel in Faith

David wrote many psalms, so did Asaph, whom he had appointed and trained as a worshipper.

David killed Goliath. His brave and mighty men killed Goliath's brother and other gigantic Philistines.

1 Chronicles 20:5-8 (ISV)
> There was also another battle against the Philistines, when Jair's son Elhanan killed Lahmi the Gittite, Goliath's brother, whose spear was as big as a weaver's beam.
>
> There was also a battle at Gath, where there was a very tall man with six fingers on each hand and six toes on each foot – for a total of 24 digits – who was a descendant of the Rephaim.
>
> When he challenged Israel, Shimei's son Jonathan, David's nephew, killed him. These descendants from the giants in Gath died at the hands of David and his servants.

10. David Blessed the Lord with All His Heart

The last reason I found was that David always gave glory to God and blessed and thanked Him – privately, as well as in the assembly.

1 Chronicles 29:10-13 & 17-18
> Therefore David blessed the LORD in the presence of all the assembly. And David said: "Blessed are You, O LORD, the God of Israel our father, forever and ever.
>
> Yours, O LORD, is the greatness and the power and the glory and the victory and the majesty, for all that is in the heavens and in the earth is Yours. Yours is the kingdom, O LORD, and You are exalted as Head above all.
>
> Both riches and honor come from You, and You rule over all. In Your hand are power and might, and in Your hand it is to make great and to give strength to all. And now we thank You, our God, and praise Your glorious name.
>
> I know, my God, that you test the heart and have pleasure in uprightness. In the uprightness of my heart I have freely offered all these things, and

now I have seen Your people, who are present here, offering freely and joyously to You.

O LORD, the God of Abraham, Isaac, and Israel, our fathers, keep forever such purposes and thoughts in the hearts of Your people, and direct their hearts toward You."

God's Covenant with David

In 2 Samuel 7:11-14&16, the Lord promised David the following:
1) That after David passes away, the Lord will make him a house.
2) The Lord will raise up his offspring after him, who will come from his body.
3) The Lord will establish his kingdom.
4) David's offspring will build a house for the name of the Lord.
5) The Lord will establish the throne of his kingdom forever.
6) The Lord will be a father to him, and he shall be to Him a son.
7) When he makes mistakes, the Lord will discipline him with a rod of men, with the stripes of the sons of men, but…
8) His steadfast love will not depart from him, as He took it from Saul.
9) David's house and his kingdom shall be made sure forever before the Lord.
10) The throne of David shall be established forever.

The Fulfillment of God's Covenant with David

Solomon, David's son, did follow him up as king and he built a temple in Jerusalem according to the specifications that David gave him.

But the true fulfillment of God's promise to David was in Jesus Christ, born from the genealogy of David.

Jesus is the builder of a spiritual temple, a body of Christ, a temple of the Holy Spirit (2 Corinthians 6:14-18, 1 Corinthians 6:19), where believers are being built up together like living stones into a spiritual sanctuary where God lives (1 Peter 2:5, Hebrews 3:1-6).

David's Mistakes

David was not perfect, but he was human and made mistakes.

1. The Consequences of David's Adultery with Bathsheba, and the Murder of Uriah

As you know, David had sent his men off to war and fell into temptation with Bathsheba, the wife of Uriah, and committed adultery with her. When she told him that she was pregnant, he sent her husband to war, so that he would be killed. Thereafter, the children of David suffered much strife, sorrow, heartache, and death.

The prophet Nathan rebuked David for what he did and declared the words of the Lord.

2 Samuel 12:10
"Now therefore the sword shall never depart from your house, because you have despised Me and have taken the wife of Uriah the Hittite to be your wife."

2. David's Sin in Having the Census

The Word says that satan incited David to number Israel (1 Chronicles 21:1).

David's successes must have made him vulnerable for temptation and satan had an opportunity to lure him into establishing the size of his kingdom.

David Requested to Rather Be Corrected by God, Than by Men

Still, David's heart was open for correction from the Lord. Furthermore, he knew people and knew God, and he chose to rather be corrected by God, and not by people.

2 Samuel 24:14 (ISV)
So David replied to Gad, "This is a very difficult choice for me to make! Let me now please fall into the hand of the LORD, since His mercy is very great, but may I never fall into human hands!"

David's Instructions to Solomon

David was a good father and a good leader and wanted to ensure that his son would be equipped to follow him up as the king.

When David's time drew near, he gave Solomon the following advice and instructions:

- To be strong, and to be a man
- To keep the instructions of the Lord and to diligently follow Him and walk in His ways, according to His values
- To know God and to serve Him wholeheartedly and willingly, for the Lord searches all hearts and understands every plan and thought
- If he seeks the Lord, then the Lord will be found by him
- He warned Solomon to be careful, because the Lord had chosen him to build a house for His sanctuary (1 Kings 2:1-4 and 1 Chronicles 28:9-10)

He gave Solomon these instructions so that he may prosper. For the Lord had promised that if his sons would pay close attention to walk before the Lord in faithfulness, with all their heart, and with all their soul, he will not lack a man on the throne of Israel.

David had wanted to build the temple for the Lord in Jerusalem, but the Lord said that because David was a man of war, He would rather that Solomon build the temple.

David made all the preparations for Solomon to build the temple. He established the plan for the temple, as well as accumulated a tremendous amount of gold, riches, and materials needed for Solomon to build the temple when his time came to reign.

When David was old, he made Solomon king over Israel (1Chronicles 23:1).

King Solomon (971 – 931 BC)

How Solomon Glorified God

Solomon started off very well in the ways of the Lord and followed his father's instructions to build the temple, the sanctuary for the Lord to live amongst His people.

God Gave Solomon Wisdom

God gave Solomon wisdom beyond measure, because he didn't ask Him for possessions, wealth, honor, or the life of those who hated him, or for a long life, but asked for wisdom to govern the Lord's people (2Chronicles 1:7-13 and 1Kings 4:29-30).

Solomon Built the Temple in Jerusalem

The Lord gave Solomon rest from his enemies on every side (1 Kings 5:3-4). In the fourth year of his reign, he started building the house of the Lord in Jerusalem on Mount Moriah, where the Lord had appeared to David his father, at the place that David had appointed (2Chronicles 3:1-2).

When all the work that Solomon did for the house of the Lord was completed, he brought in the things that David had dedicated and stored – all the silver, the gold, and all the vessels in the treasuries of the house of God (2Chronicles 5:1).

The Magnificent Glory of the Lord Filled the Temple

After completing the temple, the priests and the Levitical singers, the trumpeters and others playing on cymbals and other musical instruments, praised the Lord and gave thanks to Him with one accord.

They sang, "The Lord is good, for His steadfast love endures forever," and the house of the Lord was filled with a cloud, so that the priests could not stand to minister because of the cloud, for the glory of the LORD filled the house of God (2Chronicles 5:11-14 and 2Chronicles 7:6).

Solomon Completed the Temple as Well as the King's House

Solomon also completed the king's house. Everything that Solomon had planned to do in the house of the Lord and in his own house, he successfully accomplished (2Chronicles 7:11).

Solomon Blessed the Lord

1Kings 8:22-24 (GW)
> In the presence of the entire assembly of Israel, Solomon stood in front of the LORD'S altar. He stretched out his hands toward heaven and said, "LORD God of Israel, there is no god like You in heaven above or on earth below. You keep your promise of mercy to Your servants, who obey you wholeheartedly. You have kept Your promise to my father David, Your servant. With Your mouth You promised it. With Your hand You carried it out as it is today."

The Lord's Promise That He Will Always Be Available in the Temple

2Chronicles 7:12-16(KJV)
> And the LORD appeared to Solomon by night, and said unto him, I have heard thy prayer, and have chosen this place to Myself for an house of sacrifice. If I shut up heaven that there be no rain, or if I command the locusts to devour the land, or if I send pestilence among My people;
>
> If My people, which are called by My name, shall humble themselves, and pray, and seek My face, and turn from their wicked ways; then will I hear from heaven, and will forgive their sin, and will heal their land.
>
> Now Mine eyes shall be open, and Mine ears attent unto the prayer that is made in this place. For now have I chosen and sanctified this house, that My name may be there for ever: and Mine eyes and Mine heart shall be there perpetually.

Take notice of what the Lord is promising Solomon here, as He reveals the deep desire of His heart to live amongst His people – to be available to them, to help, advise, guide, and bless them as He pours out His loving kindness on them.

God solemnly promised that His heart, eyes and ears will be in the temple, attentive to what is asked, said, and done in the His sanctuary. Even if they couldn't see Him, He was there.

The Lord's Earnest Warning to Solomon

The Lord earnestly warned Solomon and told him what would happen if Israel would not follow Him and listen to His instructions.

1 Kings 9:4-5
> And as for you, if you will walk before Me, as David your father walked, with integrity of heart and uprightness, doing according to all that I have commanded you, and keeping My statutes and My rules, then I will establish your royal throne over Israel forever, as I promised David your father, saying, "You shall not lack a man on the throne of Israel."

The Lord warned that if Solomon would turn away from following Him, him or his children, and not keep His commandments and His statutes that He set before him, but go and serve other gods and serve them, then (1 Kings 9:6-9):

- The Lord would cut off Israel from the land that He has given them, and;
- The house that He has consecrated for His name, He would cast out of His sight, and;
- Israel would become a proverb and a byword among all peoples;
- And this house would become a heap of ruins. Everyone passing by it would be astonished and would hiss, and they would say, "Why has the Lord done thus to this land and to this house?"
- Then they would say, "Because they abandoned the Lord their God who brought their fathers out of Egypt and laid hold on other gods and worshipped them and served them;
- Therefore, the Lord has brought all this disaster on them.

Solomon Did Not Walk in the Way of the Gift of Wisdom

1 Kings 11:1-5
> Now King Solomon loved many foreign women, along with the daughter of Pharaoh: Moabite, Ammonite, Edomite, Sidonian, and Hittite women, from the nations concerning which the LORD had said to the people of Israel, "You shall not enter into marriage with them, neither shall they with you, for surely they will turn away your heart after their gods." <u>Solomon clung to these in love.</u> He had 700 wives, who were princesses, and 300 concubines. And his wives turned away his heart.
>
> For when Solomon was old <u>his wives turned away his heart after other gods, and his heart was not wholly true to the LORD his God,</u> as was the

heart of David his father. For Solomon went after Ashtoreth the goddess of the Sidonians, and after Milcom the abomination of the Ammonites.

Solomon had the gift of wisdom but stumbled and didn't walk in the way of wisdom. He didn't obey the instructions of his father David, and he didn't take to heart the warnings of the Lord and neglected the fear of the Lord.

Solomon did what was evil in the sight of the Lord and built a high place (a place of worship) for Chemosh, an idol of Moab, and for Molech, an idol of the Ammonites, on the mountain east of Jerusalem. And he did so for all his foreign wives who made offerings to their gods (1 Kings 11:6-8).

A Divided Kingdom

The consequences of Solomon's lack of walking in the way of wisdom were the divided kingdom.

1Kings 11:9-13
> And the LORD was angry with Solomon, because his heart had turned away from the LORD, the God of Israel, who had appeared to him twice and had commanded him concerning this thing that he should not go after other gods. But he did not keep what the LORD commanded. Therefore the Lord said to Solomon, "Since this has been your practice and you have not kept My covenant and My statutes that I have commanded you, I will surely tear the kingdom from you and will give it to your servant.
>
> Yet for the sake of David your father, I will not do it in your days, but I will tear it out of the hand of your son.
>
> However, I will not tear away all the kingdom, but I will give one tribe to your son, for the sake of David My servant and for the sake of Jerusalem that I have chosen."

God Remembered David

God kept His promise to David, by giving one tribe to Rehoboam, Solomon's son, *"That David My servant may always have a lamp before Me in Jerusalem, the city where I have chosen to put My Name."* (1 Kings 11:36)

Glory to Glory Q&A

1. What is your point of view on God's reaction to Solomon's idolatry?
2. What is it about David that made God choose him? Select from the following list the statements that are true:

    a. David's "happy-go-lucky" attitude
    b. His weaknesses
    c. His earnest desire to do God's will
    d. His compassion for God's people
    e. His confidence in his own ability to do warfare
    f. His confidence in his ability to manage God's people
    g. His confidence and faith in God's ability to help him
    h. He was determined to serve the Lord with all of his heart and soul

Chapter 6

What Did Kings David and Solomon Write About?

Before continuing with the history of the kings of Judah and Israel, I am going to mix up the order of your Bible a little bit and look first at what David wrote in Psalms, and what Solomon wrote in Proverbs, Ecclesiastes, and the Song of Solomon.

What was David's secret to success, and what prophecies did he receive as he sang in the Psalms about Christ, the Messiah, the anointed one, the offspring of David?

In His foreknowledge, God already knew that the earthly kings of Judah and Israel would fail to establish His kingdom in this earth.

What is becoming clearer through the history and the words of the prophets that follow is that God is starting to reveal what had been hidden from the beginning: The mystery that the Gentiles, the "people who are not called My people" will also be able to become children and heirs of God through faith in Christ, and that His kingdom will be an everlasting kingdom, and that the righteous shall live by faith.

Psalms

1. David's Secret to Success

Reading the Psalms of David is like reading his personal journal of conversations he had with the Lord.

The words of King David have moved many generations, for thousands of years, to have faith in God.

His words are not only a testimony of his own heart being wholly committed to following the Lord, but they have inspired countless believers to follow his lead and instructions to fully serve the Lord with all of their heart.

Following are some of those words to memorize, meditate, and savor on. I suggest that you visualize every detail in these scriptures as you read them; see yourself in the picture – feel what David felt, and see what David saw:

Psalms 16:7-11
> I bless the LORD who gives me counsel; in the night also my heart instructs me. I have set the LORD always before me; because He is at my right hand, I shall not be shaken. Therefore my heart is glad, and my whole being rejoices; my flesh also dwells secure. For You will not abandon my soul to Sheol, or let Your holy one see corruption. You make known to me the path of life; in Your presence there is fullness of joy; at Your right hand are pleasures forevermore."

Psalms 17:6-9
> I call upon You, for You will answer me, O God; incline Your ear to me; hear my words. Wondrously show Your steadfast love, O Savior of those who seek refuge from their adversaries at Your right hand. Keep me as the apple of Your eye; hide me in the shadow of Your wings, from the wicked who do me violence, my deadly enemies who surround me.

Psalms 18:1-3
> I love You, O LORD, my strength. The LORD is my rock and my fortress and my deliverer, my God, my rock, in whom I take refuge, my shield, and the horn of my salvation, my stronghold. I call upon the LORD, who is worthy to be praised, and I am saved from my enemies.

Psalms 18:28-36:
> For it is You who light my lamp; the LORD my God lightens my darkness. For by You I can run against a troop, and by my God I can leap over a wall.
>
> This God - His way is perfect; the word of the LORD proves true; He is a shield for all those who take refuge in Him. For who is God, but the

LORD? And who is a rock, except our God? - The God who equipped me with strength and made my way blameless.

He made my feet like the feet of a deer and set me secure on the heights. He trains my hands for war, so that my arms can bend a bow of bronze. You have given me the shield of your salvation, and Your right hand supported me, and Your gentleness made me great. You gave a wide place for my steps under me, and my feet did not slip.

Psalms 34:7
> The angel of the LORD encamps around those who fear him, and delivers them.

2. Some Messianic Prophecies in Psalms

Because the Messiah is the Son of God, He has the same character of God, the same character that God already displayed in the Old Testament:

A God who acts when called upon. A God who listens to the cries of His people. A God whose steadfast love endures forever. A God who will do anything to fight for the safety and the love of His people – that they may know Him and put their faith in Him.

You Are My Son

"You are My Son, I will make nations your heritage, and you will possess the ends of the earth." (Psalms 2:6-8)

Everything in heaven and earth is to be united under Christ, that Christ be all in all (Ephesians 1). God is also confirming His covenant with Abraham in that in him, as the father of all who believe, will all the nations be blessed.

Let the Evil of the Wicked Come to an End and May You Establish Righteousness

Psalms 9:7-8
> But the LORD sits enthroned forever; He has established His throne for justice, and He judges the world with righteousness; He judges the peoples with uprightness.

The Lord Is the Strength of the Oppressed, the Fatherless and Afflicted - Those Who Seek Him Will Not Be Lost

Psalms 9:9-10
> The LORD is a stronghold for the oppressed, a stronghold in times of trouble. And those who know Your name put their trust in You, for You, O LORD, have not forsaken those who seek You.

Psalms 10:17-18
> O LORD, You hear the desire of the afflicted; You will strengthen their heart; You will incline your ear to do justice to the fatherless and the oppressed, so that man who is of the earth may strike terror no more.

Psalms 14:2-3
> The LORD looks down from heaven on the children of man, to see if there are any who understand, who seek after God. They have all turned aside; together they have become corrupt; there is none who does good, not even one.

The last scripture Paul quoted in Romans 3:11-12 and wrote in Romans 3:23-25:
> For all have sinned and fall short of the glory of God, and are justified by His grace as a gift, through the redemption that is in Christ Jesus, whom God put forward as a propitiation by His blood, to be received by faith.

The Crucifixion of Jesus

Psalms 22 portrays Jesus' anguish on the cross, as He took not only the punishment for the sins, but also bore the rejection and the anguish of those who are lost and alone. Jesus faced many demons, conquered death, and took the keys of death and hades from satan, as He triumphed over him, and the Spirit of God raised Him from the dead!

Jesus did this that everyone, from all nations, may have a chance to never be lost, demonized, rejected and alone, but to be part of Father God's household, enjoying His love, security and protection.

Psalms 34:20 prophesied that not one of Jesus' bones will be broken.

Jesus Is the King of Glory

Psalms 24:7-10
> Lift up your heads, O gates! And be lifted up, O ancient doors, that the King of glory may come in. Who is this King of glory? The LORD, strong and mighty, the LORD, mighty in battle!

> Lift up your heads, O gates! And lift them up, O ancient doors, that the King of glory may come in. Who is this King of glory? The LORD of hosts, he is the King of glory! Selah

Pardon: The Lord Is Our Light and Salvation

It will be to the honor and glory of God's name, that He pardons guilt, that all may know how gracious and merciful He is (Psalms 25:11).

The Lord's salvation is the light to the nations, there is no reason to fear (Psalms 27:1)! In Him, all the promises of God are "Yes" and "Amen".

In Him, all the nations of the world will be blessed, as God's beacon of hope still burns brightly.

Psalms 32:1 (KJV)
> Blessed is he whose transgression is forgiven, whose sin is covered.

Psalms 33:18-22 (KJV)
> Behold, the eye of the LORD is upon them that fear him, upon them that hope in His mercy; To deliver their soul from death, and to keep them alive in famine. Our soul wait for the LORD: He is our help and our shield. For our heart shall rejoice in Him, because we have trusted in His holy name. Let thy mercy, O LORD, be upon us, according as we hope in thee.

Psalm 34:18 (ISV)
> The LORD is close to the brokenhearted, and He delivers those whose spirit has been crushed.

Psalms 34:19
> Many are the afflictions of the righteous, but the LORD delivers him out of them all.

Psalm 34:22 (ISV)
> The LORD redeems the lives of His servants and none of those who trust in Him will be held guilty.

Psalms 36:7-9
> How precious is Your steadfast love, O God! The children of mankind take refuge in the shadow of Your wings. They feast on the abundance of Your house, and You give them drink from the river of Your delights. For with You is the fountain of life; in Your light do we see light.

Psalms 145:8-9 (KJV)
> The LORD is gracious and full of compassion; slow to anger, and of great mercy. The LORD is good to all: and His tender mercies are over all His works.

Delighted to Do God's Will

Psalms 40:6-8
> In sacrifice and offering You have not delighted, but You have given Me an open ear. Burnt offering and sin offering You have not required.

Then I said, "Behold, I have come; in the scroll of the book it is written of Me: I delight to do your will, O my God; your law is within My heart." (Hebrews 10:5-7, Luke 24:44)

Betrayed by a Close Friend (Judas)

Psalms 41:9
> Even My close friend in whom I trusted, who ate My bread, has lifted his heel against Me (Also see Matthew 26:23)

Your Throne, O God, Is Forever

Psalm 45 - A prophetic love song of the sons of Korah, who were taught by David, singing praises to the King whom God has anointed with the oil of gladness beyond His companions(Hebrews 1:9).

Zeal for Your House

Psalms 69:9
> For zeal for your house has consumed Me, and the reproaches of those who reproach You have fallen on Me." (Also see John 2:17 when Jesus cleaned out the temple.)

Sit at My Right Hand – Priest Forever After the Order of Melchizedek

Psalms 110:1-2
> The LORD says to my Lord: "Sit at My right hand, until I make your enemies your footstool." The LORD sends forth from Zion your mighty scepter. Rule in the midst of Your enemies!

Psalms 110:4
> The LORD has sworn and will not change His mind, "You are a priest forever after the order of Melchizedek (meaning righteousness)."

His Righteousness and Mercy Endure Forever, Remembering the Covenant Made With Abraham

Psalms 111:3-5
> Full of splendor and majesty is His work, and His righteousness endures forever. He has caused His wondrous works to be remembered; the LORD is gracious and merciful. He provides food for those who fear Him; He remembers His covenant forever.

Psalms 111:6-9
> He has shown His people the power of His works, in giving them the inheritance of the nations. The works of His hands are faithful and just; all His precepts are trustworthy; they are established forever and ever, to be performed with faithfulness and uprightness.
>
> He sent redemption to His people; He has commanded His covenant forever. Holy and awesome is His name!

Psalms 118:19-21
> Open to me the gates of righteousness, that I may enter through them and give thanks to the LORD. This is the gate of the LORD; the righteous shall enter through it. I thank you that you have answered me and have become my salvation.

By the blood of Jesus, many are justified and made righteous to be able to enter into the throne room of God and receive grace.

The Stone That the Builders Rejected

Psalms 118:22-24
> "The stone that the builders rejected has become the cornerstone. This is the LORD's doing; it is marvelous in our eyes. This is the day that the LORD has made; let us rejoice and be glad in it."

Our Help Comes From the Lord - The Lord Surrounds His People

Psalms 121:2
> "My help comes from the LORD, who made heaven and earth."

Psalms 124:8
> "Our help is in the name of the LORD, who made heaven and earth."

Psalms 125:1-2
> "Those who trust in the LORD are like Mount Zion, which cannot be moved, but abides forever. As the mountains surround Jerusalem, so the LORD surrounds His people, from this time forth and forevermore."

The Lord's Oath to David

The Lord confirmed His oath to David that He will set one of his sons on his throne forever (Psalms 132:11-12).

Psalms 132:13-18
> For the LORD has chosen Zion; He has desired it for His dwelling place: "This is My resting place forever; here I will dwell, for I have desired it. I will abundantly bless her provisions; I will satisfy her poor with bread (Jesus declared that He is the bread of life, and those who feed on Him, shall live because of Him).
>
> Her priests I will clothe with salvation, and her saints will shout for joy. There I will make a horn to sprout for David; I have prepared a lamp for My anointed. His enemies I will clothe with shame, but on Him His crown will shine."

The Lord's Mercy and the Splendor of His Everlasting Kingdom

Psalms 138:6
> For though the LORD is high, He regards the lowly, but the haughty He knows from afar.

Psalms 140:12
> I know that the LORD will maintain the cause of the afflicted, and will execute justice for the needy.

Psalms 145:11-17
> They shall speak of the glory of Your kingdom and tell of Your power, to make known to the children of man Your mighty deeds, and the glorious splendor of Your kingdom. Your kingdom is an everlasting kingdom, and your dominion endures throughout all generations. [The LORD is faithful in all his words and kind in all his works.]
>
> The LORD upholds all who are falling and raises up all who are bowed down. The eyes of all look to You, and You give them their food in due season. You open your hand; **You** satisfy the desire of every living thing. The LORD is righteous in all His ways and kind in all His works."

Psalms 147:3
> He heals the brokenhearted and binds up their wounds.

David's Songs About God's Thoughts on Mankind

David also meditated on God's thoughts and purposes for mankind.

I am convinced that these scriptures gave him additional security and confidence in the Lord as well as whom God made him to be.

He was in awe of God's majesty and His ability to be everywhere and still being attentive to the smallest detail of his life such as the unspoken thoughts of his mind, as well as the details about an unborn child. Bear in mind that when David wrote Psalm 139, he didn't have sonar or x-ray machines. To him, it was truly magical that only God could see what the naked eye couldn't see.

1) God made man a little lower than the heavenly beings (Psalms 8:3-5)
2) God crowned man with glory and honor (Psalms 8:5)
3) God gave man dominion over the works of His hands (Psalms 8:6-9)
4) God knows everything about you and He is with you wherever you are (Psalms 139)

It is the will of God that you believe and receive who He lovingly made you to be. It is time to embrace who God made you to be. You are not who others say you are, or what circumstances made you, but you are who God says you are.

Proverbs - The Way of Wisdom

Wisdom has been with God since the beginning when He formed the earth and everything in the universe.

Solomon's success was because of the wisdom that the Lord gave him, and it made him famous.

Can you recall the incident of the mothers and their babies? After the one baby died, they came to King Solomon for wisdom to determine who should have the baby who was still alive. When he said that the baby should be cut in half, the real mother tearfully surrendered her baby to the other woman to save its life. That is wisdom (1 Kings 3:16-28).

Wisdom is to be able to give counsel, to supply a solution, with God as its source.

How privileged are we to have wisdom as one of the gifts of the Holy Spirit! God gives wisdom to whomever ask it of Him, without finding fault (James 1:5).

Following are a few pearls of wisdom that Solomon wrote in Proverbs:

Receive and Treasure God's Words, Instructions and Correction

Proverbs 2:1-5 (GW)
My son, if you take My words to heart and treasure My commands within you, if you pay close attention to wisdom, and let your mind reach for understanding, if indeed you call out for insight, if you ask aloud for understanding, if you search for wisdom as if it were money and hunt for it as if it were hidden treasure, then you will understand the fear of the LORD and you will find the knowledge of God.

Proverbs 3:11-12 (GW)
Do not reject the discipline of the LORD, my son, and do not resent His warning, because the LORD warns the one He loves, even as a father warns a son with whom he is pleased. (See also Hebrews 12:5-11)

Wisdom and Discretion Are Life for Your Soul

Proverbs 3:21-22

My son, do not lose sight of these – keep sound wisdom and discretion, and they will be life for your soul and adornment for your neck.

Wisdom Will Keep You From Stumbling and From Fear

Proverbs 3:23-26 (GW)
> Then you will go safely on your way, and you will not hurt your foot. When you lie down, you will not be afraid. As you lie there, your sleep will be sweet. Do not be afraid of sudden terror or of the destruction of wicked people when it comes. The LORD will be your confidence. He will keep your foot from getting caught.

Walk With the Wise and Follow the Way of Insight

Proverbs 9:5-6 (GW)
> Come, eat My bread, and drink the wine I have mixed. Stop being gullible and live. Start traveling the road to understanding.

Proverbs 13:20 (KJV)
> He that walketh with wise men shall be wise: but a companion of fools shall be destroyed.

The Fear of the Lord Is a Fountain of Life

Proverbs 14:26-27 (KJV)
> In the fear of the LORD is strong confidence: and his children shall have a place of refuge. The fear of the LORD is a fountain of life, to depart from the snares of death.

Proverbs 15:16 (KJV)
> Better is little with the fear of the LORD than great treasure and trouble therewith.

Take Ownership of Your Own Mistakes and Choices, Fear the Lord

Proverbs 16:25 (KJV)
> There is a way that seemeth right unto a man, but the end thereof are the ways of death.

Proverbs 16:2-3
> All the ways of a man are pure in his own eyes, but the LORD weighs the spirit. Commit your work to the LORD, and your plans will be established.

Proverbs 19:3
> When a man's folly brings his way to ruin, his heart rages against the LORD.

Let the Dross Be Removed, and Your Fountain Be Made Clear

Proverbs 25:4-5
> Take away the dross from the silver, and the smith has material for a vessel; take away the wicked from the presence of the king, and his throne will be established in righteousness.

Proverbs 25:26 (ISV)
> A muddied spring or a polluted well – that's what a righteous person is who compromises with the wicked.

Ecclesiastes

Ecclesiastes 3:1-2
> For everything there is a season, and a time for every matter under heaven: a time to be born, and a time to die; a time to plant, and a time to pluck up what is planted;

About seven hundred years after Solomon, Jesus taught that a man (or woman) who hears the word and does it, is like a man building his house on a rock, by digging deep and applying the word to his own life. When the storms come, the house will remain standing. If one does not apply the Word to their life, it's like building a house on sand and when the storms come, the house is destroyed (Luke 6:46-49).

Another one of Jesus' warnings was given to those who flow in the gifts of the Holy Spirit, but are pursuing evil, when He said in Matthew 7:21-23:

> Not everyone who says to Me, 'Lord, Lord,' will enter the kingdom of heaven, <u>but the one who does the will of My Father</u> who is in heaven. On that day many will say to Me, 'Lord, Lord, did we not prophesy in Your name, and cast out demons in Your name, and do many mighty works in Your name?' And then will I declare to them, 'I never knew you; <u>depart from Me, you workers of evil and lawlessness</u>.'

Wisdom advises one to follow the instruction of one's father. David earnestly advised Solomon to follow the Lord with all his heart and to walk in His ways. Furthermore, wisdom begins with the fear of the Lord – to reverently seek His counsel and obey His voice.

After Solomon had completed the temple and the palace, he turned away from the Lord by marrying hundreds of foreign women and building their idols and serving their gods with them – something the Lord had earnestly warned him not to do!

Because of Solomon's unfaithfulness to the Lord, Israel was divided into two tribes and eventually taken into captivity. But the Lord had mercy and a remnant was saved and returned later to Jerusalem. From this remnant, the Messiah was born so that all who believe in Him may be saved!

When reading Ecclesiastes, Solomon starts off by calling everything vanity, meaning worthless and futile. To me, this has more an aroma of bitterness and resentment than of faith, hope, or love.

Bitterness will destroy one's faith, hope, and love, that is why the Lord warned about it (Deuteronomy 29:18). When David was confronted with bitter people, he chose to rather strengthen himself in the Lord (1 Samuel 30:6).

Had Solomon chosen to follow the instructions of his father, who knows, maybe the history of Israel would have developed differently.

Song of Solomon

After Solomon brokenly wrote in Ecclesiastes 7:20 that *"there is not a righteous man on earth, who does good and never sins,"* he mercifully prophesied about the glory of Christ's love for His bride in Song of Solomon.

The bride would look to Christ for answers and strength.

Song of Solomon 4:9
> You have captivated My heart, My sister, My bride; <u>you have captivated My heart with one glance of your eyes</u>, with one jewel of your necklace.

And the bride in turn sings her praises to her Beloved Savior (based on Song of Solomon 5:10-16, paraphrased):

My Beloved is holy, bright shining like the sun, His clothes stained with blood, seated high above all powers, principalities and all wickedness, in glorious strength and in majesty.

His eyes are filled with love and peace from rivers of living waters, bubbling up from Father God's deep source of life.

His anointing drips with healing and His Words have power to make the dead come to life! In His presence is fullness of joy.

His hands bear the marks of His perfect offering out of love for His bride, and His body bears the marks of the lashes for sin that He would take upon Himself, because He loves her.

Where He walks, there is life, and He fills all in all. His glory is pure and fragrant and beautiful. There is none like Him in all creation.

This is my Beloved, and this is my Friend, daughters of Jerusalem.

Glory to Glory Q&A

1. Memorize and meditate on David's "secrets for success" that he recorded in Psalms. You are welcome to add to the list!
2. Meditate on Psalms 8 and 139.
3. Look at the list of fears below and see if there are any that you are struggling with.
   Then choose any of the scriptures written by David to memorize and meditate on, so that you dismantle the fear and build up faith based on God's truth in its place.
   a. Fear of missing out
   b. Fear of failure
   c. Fear of people – deep-rooted people pleasing or approval-seeking from people
   d. Fear of calamity
   e. Fear of poverty
   f. Fear of death
   g. Fear of not being good enough
   h. Fear of punishment
   i. Fear of being loved
   j. Fear of rejection

Like David, it is better to be consumed by knowing God, than to be consumed by anxiety or fear.

Knowing God displaces fears and anxiety by having faith in Him.

Chapter 7

The Divided Kingdom, Prophets Jonah, Amos and Hosea

Don't Stop Reading Yet

Don't stop reading now! Our movie is not finished yet!

You might think that reading through these lists of kings, events, and prophecies is boring, but ask yourself these questions:

- Why did God have all this information recorded in the Bible for us to read?
- What could possibly be the value of reading about these "historic" events?
- It is written in Ephesians 1 that Christ came at the appointed time. Why? Why did it take so long before God sent His Son to save the world?

God gave the people what they asked for. They wanted a king to "fight for them", even when God was their king and He was fighting for them.

Since Adam and Eve, God wanted to drive these points home:

- He alone is God of heaven and earth, and He has your best interests at heart.
- He wants to be your Savior, and the one who fights your battles!

- When He tells you not to do something – it is to protect you and to keep you safe.

God was preparing the way for His kingdom to be established in the hearts and minds of His people to help them in their daily lives.

He made you to see, to feel, to touch, to laugh, and to cry... like He does. It is His design. His desire is for you to live gloriously with every fiber of your being – in your heart, soul, body and spirit.

We can read all these events about Israel and Judah, Adam and Eve, and be all judgmental and say that we would never have disobeyed God's instructions or served other gods.

But don't be so sure of that. For we all have flesh, and our idols might simply have different shapes and sizes.

What I believe the Lord has taught me is that unless the flesh sees and feels the consequences of rejecting God, and of not hearing and not obeying His voice, it won't surrender to Christ's authority. Sad but true.

God even had to strike Saul with blindness and speak to him in a clear voice, to stop him in his tracks and get him to turn from killing Christians, to serving God!

These "boring lists" have the power to save lives.

Pay Close Attention

Pay close attention to how people followed or rejected God's instructions and warnings.

Listen intently to the Lord's words spoken through His prophets and notice His actions and assess in your heart where you're at.

Consider while you are reading: What if you were king (or queen) of Judah or Israel – what would you have done? How would <u>you</u> have responded to God's instructions and how would <u>you</u> have led God's people?

What do you think queen Esther would have done if she was queen of Israel...?

These Bible events are all about God's love and His earnest desire for people to have faith in Him.

If you read what the kings did, you'll understand the context of what God was talking about through the prophets as He sent them to the kings of the day to bring correction, direction and decrees of God's future plans.

Much of what the prophets wrote about had to do with what the people did at the time and how God reacted to those circumstances.

When reading the prophecies and decrees about the Messiah, the outpouring of the Holy Spirit and God's Kingdom, you will understand the context of why God gave the incredible gifts of salvation and grace to mankind and I won't be surprised if you fall in love with God all over again.

When one is a child, one is more concerned and obsessed with having one's own needs met. A child usually does not have the insight into their parents' feelings, emotions, circumstances or motives. It is when you mature or become a parent yourself that you gain more insight into the love, sacrifices, commitment and challenges it takes to be a good parent.

Receiving insight into what brought God sorrow, and how He gave His everything to save the world, could catapult you into becoming more spiritually mature.

The Two Kingdoms

The Bible books of Kings and Chronicles describe the history of Israel and Judah during the divided kingdom.

- Judah was known as the Southern Kingdom, in Jerusalem
- Israel was known as the Northern Kingdom, in Shechem, Tirzah or Samaria as times went by

The Timeline

I have included a timeline (that I've compiled for myself, but thought you'd also find handy) to see how the kings of Judah and Israel reigned side by side, and when each group went into exile.

The timeline also shows the prophets who prophesied during the reign of the kings.

About the Dates

There is some discussion on the dates and years in the Bible. Just from the looks of it, the math doesn't always seem to add up.

A person called Edwin R. Thiele researched some inconsistencies regarding the timelines of Israel and Judah. He explained that differences are due to 1) co-regencies (of sons and fathers where their reigns sometimes overlapped), and 2) differences in calculation methods, as well as 3) the calendars in Judah and Israel having a difference of six months.

The dates I use, are from *RW Research Inc, published in 2005 by Rose publishers*. The dates were used to put scriptures and history chronologically into context to give better understanding and insight, to know God more intimately. I firmly believe that a few years here and there due to human differences truly don't change who God is.

A Timeline of Kings and Prophets of the Divided Kingdom

Prophet	Kings of Judah	Kings of Israel	Prophet
	Rehoboam, reigned 17years (931-913) Abijah (18th year of Jeroboam) reigned 3years (913-911) Asa (20th year of Jeroboam) reigned 41 years (911-870)	Jeroboam, reigned 22years (931-910) Nadab (2nd year of Asa) reigned 2 years (910-909) Baasha (3rd year of Asa) reigned 24 years (909 – 886) Elah (26th year of Asa) reigned 2 years (886-885) Zimri (27th year of Asa) reigned 7 days Omri (31st year of Asa) reigned 12 years (885-874) Ahab (38th year of Asa) reigned 22years (874-853)	Elijah (870-845)
	Jehoshaphat (4th year of Ahab) reigned 25 years (873-848) Jehoram, reigned 8 years (853-841) Ahazia (12th year of Joram) reigned 1 year (841) Athalia, reigned 7 years (841-835) Joash (reigned for 40 years (835-796)	Ahaziah (17th year of Jehoshaphat) reigned 2years (853-852) Joram/Jehoram, 18th year of Jehoshaphat, reigned 12 years (852-841) Jehu, reigned 28 years (841-814) Jehoahaz, (814-798) Jehoash (798-782)	Elisha (845-800) Jonah (781)
Isaiah (760-673)	Amaziah, reigned 29years (796-767) Azariah/Uzziah (in 27th year of Jeroboam) – reigned 52 years (792-740)	Jeroboam II (15th year of Amazia) reigned 41 years (793-753) Zechariah (in 38th year of Azariah) reigned 6 months (753) Shallum (in 39th year of Uzzia/Azariah) reigned 1 month (752)	Amos (765-754) Hosea (758-725)
Micah (738-698)	Jotham (in 2nd year of Pekah) reigned 16years (750-732) Ahaz (in 17th year of Pekah) reigned for 16 years (735-716) Hezekiah (in 3rd year of Hoshea) reigned 29 years (716-687)	Menahem (in 39th year of Azariah) reigned 10 years (752-742) Pekahiah (in 50th year of Azariah) reigned 2 years (742-740) Pekah (in 52nd year of Azariah) reigned 20years (752-732)	
Jeremiah (650-582) Zephaniah (640-626) Ezekiel (620-570) Daniel (620-540)	Manasseh (reign for 55years (697-643) Amon (reigned for 2 years) (643-641) Josiah (reigned 31 years (641-609) Jehoahaz, reigned 3 months (609) Eliakim/Jehoiakim – reigned 11 years (609-598) First exile of Jews to Babylon (605) Jehoiachin (Jeconiah) (598-597) Zedekiah (Jehoiakim's brother – made king by Nebuchadnezzar), for 11years. (597-586) Judah's exile to Babylon. (580 BC)	Hoshea (in 12th year of Ahaz) reigned 9 years (732-722) Israel falls to Assyrians. (722 BC)	Nahum (658-615)

A Summary of the Kings of Israel (931BC to 722BC)

90 percent of the kings of Israel turned away from the Lord to worship idols.

Because of their unfaithfulness to the Lord, they led God's people away from serving Him. They caused Israel to worship other gods who had absolutely no power or ability to help them, for the gods they were serving were actually the works of their own hands!

Jeroboam I was Solomon's servant who reigned for 22 years and built Shechem. He made two calves of gold, thinking in his heart that the people would return to Rehoboam, king of Judah, when they went to offer sacrifices to the Lord in Jerusalem, and that they would kill him. He caused the people to perform this sin. He made temples on high places and appointed priests from among all the people, who were not of the Levites. He cast the Lord behind his back.

Nadab, Baasha and Elah all did evil, following in the ways of Jeroboam.

Zimri destroyed the house of Baasha according to the word of the Lord by Jehu the prophet, because of the sins of Elah and Baasha. They sinned and caused Israel to sin, provoking the Lord to anger by their idols. He also walked in the way of Jeroboam.

Omri bought the hill of Samaria. He did more evil than all before him, and walked in the ways of Jeroboam.

Ahab did more evil than all who were before him. He took Jezebel, the daughter of Ethbaal, king of the Sidonians, as wife, and went to serve Baal and worshipped him. He erected an altar for Baal in the house of Baal, and he made an Asherah. He did more to provoke the Lord to anger than all the kings before him. In his days Hiel of Bethel, built Jericho. He laid the foundation at the cost of his firstborn. He set up its gates at the cost of his youngest son, according to the word of the Lord that He spoke by Joshua whereby the Lord instructed that Jericho should never be rebuilt.

The prophet Elijah (870-845) had faith and absolute confidence in the Lord. The Lord defeated the prophets of Baal when He set fire to the altar, the bull, the wood and everything on it that were all drenched in water! The Lord's fire consumed the burnt offering, the wood, the stones, and the dust, and licked up the water that was in the trench! Elijah slaughtered the prophets of Baal.

Jezebel schemed to get Naboth stoned in order for Ahab to take possession of Naboth's vineyard. Then the Lord sent Elijah with a word about the disaster that would come as a result of their sins. Then Ahab repented. The Lord showed mercy to him because Ahab humbled himself before the Lord, and He told Elijah that the disaster would not come in the days of Ahab, but in his son's days. When the king died, the dogs licked up his blood and the prostitutes washed themselves in it, according to the word that the Lord had spoken.

Ahaziah, followed by Joram/Jehoram both did evil, but the latter took away the pillar of Baal.

Jehu was anointed by Elisha to destroy all the evil that Ahab had done. He killed Ahazia, Joram and all the Baal prophets. He wiped out Baal from Israel. However, he did not keep the law nor walk in the ways of the Lord with all his heart.

Thereafter, Jehoash and then Jeroboam II reigned and both did evil.

Zechariah reigned for six months and did evil. The promise that God made to Jehu that his sons shall sit on the throne up to four generations came to pass, for God is faithful.

Shallum reigned for one month and was struck down by Menahem who also did evil. He exacted silver and money from Israel to give to Pul, king of Assyria.

Pekahiah reigned for two years and also did evil. So did Pekah who reigned for 20 years and followed the sins of Jeroboam. King Tiglath-pileser of Assyria came, captured six cities, of which Gilead, Galilee and Naphtali, and carried people captive to Assyria.

Hoshea reigned for nine years and did evil, yet not as the kings before him.

The King of Assyria found treachery in King Hoshea and bound him up in prison. Then he invaded all the land and besieged Samaria for three years (in 9th year of Hoshea and 6th year of Hezekiah). He carried the Israelites away to Assyria (722 BC) and placed them in Halah, and on the Habor, the river of Gozan, and in the cities of the Medes, because the Israelites neither listened to, nor obeyed the Lord (2 Kings 17:6-23).

The King of Assyria brought people from Babylon, Cuthah, Ava, Hamath, and Sepharvaim, and placed them in the cities of Samaria instead of Israel. They served their own gods, and also tried to serve the Lord, but didn't give up their own gods. They didn't fear the Lord (2 Kings 17:24-41).

A Summary of the Kings of Judah (931BC – 586 BC)

Half of the kings of Judah turned away from the Lord to worship idols, leading the Lord's people astray.

Rehoboam, the son of Solomon did evil and provoked the Lord to jealousy, more than all of their fathers had done. They built for themselves high places, pillars, and Asherim on every hill and under every green tree, and there were also male cult prostitutes.

They did according to all the abominations of the nations that the Lord drove out before the people of Israel. He took away the treasures of the house of the Lord and the treasures of the king's house. There was war between Rehoboam and Jeroboam continually.

Abijah walked in all the sins of Rehoboam, but for David's sake, the Lord gave him a lamp in Jerusalem.

Asa reigned for 41 years and did what was right, as David did. He put away the male cult prostitutes and removed all the idols that his father Abijah had made. He also removed his mother from being queen mother because she had made an abominable image for Asherah, but the high places were not taken down. The heart of Asa was wholly true to the Lord all his days.

Jehoshaphat started reigning in the fourth year of Ahab, king of Israel. He started off well by walking in the way of Asa and serving the Lord, yet he didn't take down the high places. He also made peace with the king of Israel. From the land he also exterminated the remnant of the male cult prostitutes who had remained. Then he joined with king Ahaziah of Israel, who acted wickedly.

Jehoram (Joram), the son of Jehoshaphat reigned for eight years, took the daughter of Ahab as his wife and did evil. His youngest son, Ahaziah, reigned for one year and did evil as he walked in the ways of Ahab.

Athaliah, the mother of Ahaziah, reigned for seven years. She destroyed the royal family. Then Jehosheba, her sister, took Joash, the son of Ahaziah and hid him for six years so that he was not put to death, while Athaliah reigned. Wicked Athaliah broke into the house of the Lord and stole all the things of the Lord for the Baals.

Joash (Jehoash), the son of Athaliah, started reigning when he was seven years old and reigned for 40 years. He did what was right in the eyes of the Lord while the priest Jehoiada was alive. He restored the house of the Lord. After Jehoiada died, he listened to princes of Judah and abandoned the house of the Lord and served Asherim and idols. When Zechariah, Jehoiada's son, came with a word from the Lord, Joash killed him.

Joash's son, Amaziah, as well as the following two generations of kings, Azariah (also known as Uzziah) and Jotham did what was right in the eyes of the Lord, yet not like David. They did not remove the high places and people still made offerings there.

Ahaz (also known as Jehoahaz), the son of Jotham, did not do what was right. He even burned his son as an offering, according to the despicable practices of the nations that the Lord drove out before the people of Israel!

He sacrificed and made offerings on high places and under every green tree. He took silver and gold from the house of the Lord to give to the king of Assyria.

Hezekiah did what was right and removed the high places, broke pillars, and cut down the Asherah. He held fast to the Lord like none of the kings of Judah before him. The Lord was with him. He rebelled against the king of Assyria and would not serve him.

In the 14th year of Hezekiah, Sennacherib, king of Assyria came up against fortified cities of Judah and took them. Hezekiah made a deal with the king of Syria and gave him all the silver that was found in the house of the Lord and in the treasuries of the king's house. He stripped the gold from the doors of the temple of the Lord, and from the doorposts and gave it to the foreign king.

King Sennacherib of Assyria defied the Lord by telling Hezekiah a lie about God. Hezekiah prayed and the Lord brought a prophecy through Isaiah, of Sennacherib's fall, and also that a remnant out of the house of Judah shall again take root downward and bear fruit upward (2 Kings 19).

Manasseh, the son of Hezekiah, started reigning at age 12 and reigned for 55 years. He did much evil, provoking the Lord to anger. He rebuilt high places and erected altars for Baal and Asherah, as Ahab did. He even built altars in the house of the Lord, and also built altars for all the hosts of heaven in the two courts of the house of the Lord. He burned his son as an offering, used fortune-telling and omens, dealt with mediums, and with necromancers.

He also made a carved image of Asherah and set it in the house of the Lord, the temple that Solomon built according to the specifications that the Lord gave to David. Manasseh made Judah sin greatly with all his abominations and shed a lot of innocent blood by his atrocities. That is why the Lord brought much disaster upon Jerusalem for the sanctuary of the Lord was the place of intimacy where He lived amongst His people.

Amon also did much evil as his father Manasseh. He abandoned the Lord and did not walk in the way of the Lord.

Josiah, Amon's son, started reigning from age eight and he reigned for 31 years. He did what was right in the eyes of the Lord and walked in the ways of David. He broke down Baals, and Asherim, idols and images. He found the book of the law, repaired the temple, and kept the Passover. He did not listen to the words of Neco, from the mouth of God, and was killed in battle.

Jehoahaz (Shallum), the son of Josiah, started reigning at age 23 and reigned for three months. Then the king of Egypt removed him from office in Jerusalem.

Eliakim, the brother of the king of Egypt, changed his name to Jehoiakim and reigned for 11 years, while doing evil. Nebuchadnezzar, the king of Babylon, came up against him and bound him in chains to take him, as well as vessels of the house of the Lord, to Babylon.

Zedekiah, Jehoiakim's brother, was made king by Nebuchadnezzar at the age of 21 and reigned for 11 years. He did evil and did not humble himself before the prophet Jeremiah who spoke from the mouth of the Lord but stiffened his neck and hardened his heart.

Because of all the abominations and disobedience of Judah, God raised up the king of the Chaldeans and gave them into his hand. They burned the house of the Lord and broke down the wall of Jerusalem and burned all its palaces with fire and destroyed all its previous vessels.

Judah was taken to exile in Babylon in 586 BC and became servants until the establishment of the kingdom of Persia, to fulfill a prophecy by Jeremiah, to fulfill 70 years (2 Chronicles 36:14-21).

The Lord's Prophets

The prophets were more than a voice of God to the people. They were giving God's heart to the people. They were to bring His Name, His character, to the people, for they were appointed by God to speak on His behalf.

God's words are a map to His heart, for Jesus said that out of the fullness of the heart, the mouth speaks.

I have included many of God's words as written in the books of the prophets so that you may hear directly from God as He spoke thousands of years ago.

For God, one day is like a thousand years. What He valued way back when, He still holds dear today.

Old Testament Prophets

In the Old Testament, the prophets didn't have the indwelling of the Holy Spirit as is the case from the New Testament onwards.

The prophets who were appointed by God had the Holy Spirit come upon them and then they spoke with clarity, word for word what God said. It was as if they didn't have the ability to filter God's words but were able to say exactly what God said. Many of these prophets prophesied from having an encounter with God first, like Isaiah, Jeremiah, and Ezekiel.

These three prophets have each written down their encounters with God:

Isaiah described seeing the throne of God during the days of King Uzziah. He saw the Lord high and lifted up and the train of His robe filling the temple. Then the Lord commissioned him to speak on His behalf (Isaiah 6:1-13).

Jeremiah was only a youth when the Lord called him, encouraging him to speak what He told him to speak (Jeremiah 1:4-10). Jeremiah received many prophetic symbols in his encounters with the Lord, like for instance, the almond branch, which meant that the Lord is watching over His word to perform it (Jeremiah 1:11-12).

Ezekiel starts by describing the stormy wind, the great cloud, flashing fire, the four living creatures, and the likeness of the throne and the glory of the Lord. Then the Lord spoke to him as he was having this spiritual encounter with the Lord, and He called Ezekiel to speak on His behalf to the people (Ezekiel 1-2).

There were also many false prophets. The books of Jeremiah and Ezekiel elaborate on those who deliberately "prophesied" what the people wanted to hear, and not what God said. Those false prophets were speaking from their own hearts and minds, even using words that they heard from others and not by the Holy Spirit - but I will share more about them later.

Let's get back to the chronological sequence of events.

Jonah (781 BC)

Jonah's Instruction to Go to Nineveh

I was really blessed when I discovered the point in time that the Lord had sent Jonah to Nineveh and where it fit into Israel's history. For once again, the Lord's mercy and steadfast love are proven true!

Nineveh was the capital of Assyria. Amidst Judah and Israel's unfaithfulness, the Lord sent Jonah to Nineveh to tell them that their evil deeds have become known and that they should turn away from them.

Jonah rebelled against going, because he knew that the Lord was merciful and would forgive Nineveh should they repent and turn away from doing evil. That was the reason that Jonah first went to Tarshish, in the opposite direction of Nineveh. The Lord had to go to great lengths (remember the incident with the fish), to get Jonah to Nineveh to deliver His message (Jonah 1-2).

After Jonah had delivered the Lord's message to Nineveh, they repented from evil and believed God. Then God kept the disaster from them that He said He would do to them (Jonah 3:5-10).

Jonah's Anger Because of God's Mercy

Jonah was very disappointed and angry with the Lord. He argued with God, saying that he knew all along that God would forgive them because He is merciful, gracious, slow to anger, and abounding in steadfast love (Jonah 4:1-4).

Then the Lord told Jonah, "Do you do well to be angry?"

God Teaches Jonah the Value of People

Jonah went out of the city and made a shelter for himself there. He sat under it in the shade, to see what would become of the city.

The Lord made a plant to come up over Jonah, that he could sit in its shade and be comfortable. Jonah was very glad because of the plant, but at dawn the next day, God sent a worm that attacked the plant, so that it died.

When the sun rose, God sent a scorching wind, and the sun beat down on Jonah's head so that he felt weak. Jonah asked that he might die (Jonah 4:5-8).

Jonah 4:9-11
> But God said to Jonah, "Do you do well to be angry for the plant?" And he said, "Yes, I do well to be angry, angry enough to die."
>
> And the LORD said, "You pity the plant, for which you did not labor, nor did you make it grow, which came into being in a night and perished in a night. And should not I pity Nineveh, that great city, in which there are more than 120,000 persons who do not know their right hand from their left, and also much cattle?"

God's Foreknowledge

Not only did God prove to be merciful, but according to the timelines, He also proved to remain faithful amidst Israel's unfaithfulness.

He knew already (He is God, right?) that Israel would be taken captive to Assyria. It seems to me that He prepared the way for His beloved once again, in the same way that He provided an outcome for Israel when He had sent Joseph to Egypt ahead of time so that there would be provision and a safe place for His people in times of distress.

As the Egyptians became Israel's oppressors, so the Assyrians would as well.

Amos (765-754 BC)

Amos was prophet during the days of King Uzziah of Judah, and Jeroboam, king of Israel. He gave word for Israel's neighbors, as well as to Judah for their lies and unfaithfulness, and to Israel.

About Israel, some of the things he said were that they sold the righteous for silver and the needy for a pair of sandals.

They trampled the poor into the dust, and that a man and his father went into the same woman so that the Lord's holy name is profaned, which means "to drag God's name through the mud" in great disrespect and dishonor (Amos 2).

God First Reveals to His Prophets

Amos announced that God does nothing without first revealing His secret to His servants the prophets (Amos 3:7).

Seek the Lord and Live

Amos 5:1-5
> Hear this word that I take up over you in lamentation, O house of Israel: "Fallen, no more to rise, is the virgin Israel; forsaken on her land, with none to raise her up."

> For thus says the Lord GOD: "The city that went out a thousand shall have a hundred left, and that which went out a hundred shall have ten left to the house of Israel."

> For thus says the Lord to the house of Israel:

> "Seek Me and live; but do not seek Bethel, and do not enter into Gilgal or cross over to Beersheba; for Gilgal shall surely go into exile, and Bethel shall come to nothing."

They Trampled on the Poor

Amos 5:11-12
> "Therefore because you trample on the poor and you exact taxes of grain from him, you have built houses of hewn stone, but you shall not dwell in them; you have planted pleasant vineyards, but you shall not drink their wine.

> For I know how many are your transgressions and how great are your sins – you who afflict the righteous, who take a bribe, and turn aside the needy in the gate."

Seek Good, Hate Evil

Amos 5:13-15
"Therefore he who is prudent will keep silent in such a time, for it is an evil time. Seek good, and not evil, that you may live; and so the LORD, the God of hosts, will be with you, as you have said. Hate evil, and love good, and establish justice in the gate; it may be that the LORD, the God of hosts, will be gracious to the remnant of Joseph."

Israel Gave Offerings to the Lord, While Also Serving Idols!

Amos 5:21-27
"I hate, I despise your feasts, and I take no delight in your solemn assemblies. Even though you offer me your burnt offerings and grain offerings, I will not accept them; and the peace offerings of your fattened animals, I will not look upon them.

Take away from Me the noise of your songs; to the melody of your harps I will not listen. But let justice roll down like waters, and righteousness like an ever-flowing stream.

Did you bring to Me sacrifices and offerings during the forty years in the wilderness, O house of Israel? You shall take up Sikkuth your king, and Kiyyun your star-god – your images that you made for yourselves, and I will send you into exile beyond Damascus," says the LORD, whose name is the God of hosts.

Misery to Those Who Do Not See the Harmful Condition of God's People

Amos 6:4-8 (GW)
"How horrible it will be for those who sleep on ivory beds. They sprawl out on their couches and eat lambs from their flocks and calves from their stalls. How horrible it will be for those who make up songs as they strum a harp. Like David, they write all kinds of songs for themselves.

How horrible it will be for those who drink wine by the jugful. They rub the finest oils all over themselves and are not sorry for the ruin of the descendants of Joseph.

That is why they will now be the first to go into exile. The celebrating of those sprawled around the banquet table will stop.

The Almighty LORD has sworn an oath on Himself. The LORD God of Armies declares: I am disgusted with Jacob's pride, and I hate his palaces. So I will hand over the city and everything in it."

A Terrible Famine of Hearing the Words of the Lord

Amos 8:11-14 (GW)

"The days are going to come," declares the Almighty LORD, "when I will send a famine throughout the land. It won't be an ordinary famine or drought. Instead, there will be a famine of hearing the words of the LORD.

People will wander from sea to sea and roam from the north to the east, searching for the word of the LORD. But they won't find it.

On that day beautiful young women and strong young men will faint because of their thirst.

How horrible it will be for those who swear by Ashimah, the idol of Samaria, and say, 'I solemnly swear, Dan, as your god lives... I solemnly swear as long as there is a road to Beersheba....' Those who say this will fall and never get up again."

Israel Will Be Shaken, the Proud Removed, and the Humble Restored

Amos 9:9-12 (ISV)

"Look! I'm giving the order: I will sift the house of Israel throughout all the nations, as one sifts with a sieve, yet not a single kernel will reach the ground!

All sinners among My people will die by the sword, especially all who are saying, 'Disaster will not come upon or conquer us!'

At that time I will restore David's fallen tent, restoring its torn places. I will restore its ruins, rebuilding it as it was long ago, so My people may inherit the remnant of Edom and all of the nations that bear My name," declares the LORD who is bringing this about.

The Lord's Promise of Continuous Blessing to Come

Amos 9:13-15 (ISV)

"Look! The days are coming," declares the LORD, "when the one who sows will overtake the harvester and the treader of grapes will overtake the planter. Fresh wine will drip down from the mountains, cascading down from the hills.

I will surely restore My people Israel; they will rebuild the ruined cities and inhabit them. They will plant vineyards and drink the wine from them. They will plant gardens and eat the fruit from them.

I will plant the people of Israel in their own land, never again to be torn out of their land that I gave them," says the LORD your God.

Hosea (758-725 BC)

Hosea was a prophet during the days of Kings Uzziah, Jotham, Ahaz and Hezekiah of Judah, and in the days of king Jeroboam of Israel.

The Lord pleaded with His beloved Israel to turn away from behaving like a prostitute with other gods, and to become faithful to Him.

God told Hosea to take a prostitute as a wife, because the Lord's beloved Israel was acting like a whore towards the Lord, so that Hosea could relate and prophesy appropriately.

Israel's Unfaithfulness and Its Consequences

Hosea 2:8-13 (ISV)
"She didn't recognize that it was I who provided her grain, wine, and oil, and it was I who gave her silver, while they crafted gold for Baal.

Therefore I'll return and take back My grain at harvest time and My new wine in its season. I'll take back My wool and My flax that was to have covered her nakedness.

So now I'll reveal her lewdness to the eyes of her lovers, and no man will rescue her from My control.

I'll put a stop to her mirth, along with her celebrations, her New Moons, her Sabbaths, and all of her festive assemblies.

I'll destroy her vines and her fig trees, about which she said, 'These are the earnings that my lovers paid me. I'll make them grow into a forest, and the wild animals will eat from them.'

I'll punish her for the time she has devoted to the Baals, to whom she burned incense, and for whom she put on her earrings and jewels so she could go after her lovers and forget Me," declares the LORD.

Then the Lord Perseveres With Mercy and Loving Kindness Towards Israel

Hosea 2:14-19 (ISV)
"Therefore, look! I will now allure her. I will make her go out to the wilderness, and will speak to her heart.

There I will restore her vineyards to her, and the Valley of Achor will become a doorway to hope. There she will respond as she did in her youth, when she came up from Egypt.

It will come about at that time," declares the LORD, "that you will address Me as 'my Husband,' and you will no longer call me 'my Master'."

I will remove the names of the Baals from her vocabulary – they will not be remembered by their names anymore.

I will make a covenant with them at that time, a covenant with the wild animals of the field, with the birds of the air, and with the creatures of the ground. I will banish the battle bow, the sword, and war from the earth. I will cause My people to lie down where it is safe.

I will make you My wife forever – I will make you My wife in a way that is righteous, in a manner that is just, by a love that is gracious, and by a motive that is mercy."

Hosea Declares the Period After the Kings

Hosea 3:4-5 (KJV)
> For the children of Israel shall abide many days without a king, and without a prince, and without a sacrifice, and without an image, and without an ephod, and without teraphim:

> Afterward shall the children of Israel return, and seek the LORD their God, and David their king; and shall fear the LORD and His goodness in the latter days.

Destroyed for a Lack of Knowledge of Faithfulness and Love

Hosea 4:1-2
> Hear the word of the LORD, O children of Israel, for the LORD has a controversy with the inhabitants of the land. There is no faithfulness or steadfast love, and no knowledge of God in the land; there is swearing, lying, murder, stealing, and committing adultery; they break all bounds, and bloodshed follows bloodshed.

Hosea 4:6
> "My people are destroyed for lack of knowledge; because you have rejected knowledge, I reject you from being a priest to Me. And since you have forgotten the law of your God, I also will forget your children."

"I Desire Love"

Hosea 6:4-6
> "What shall I do with you, O Ephraim? What shall I do with you, O Judah? Your love is like a morning cloud, like the dew that goes early away.

> Therefore I have hewn (meaning to chop like an axe, to chisel, to take away that which is not of God) them by the prophets; I have slain them by the words of My mouth, and My judgment goes forth as the light.

For I desire steadfast love and not sacrifice, the knowledge of God rather than burnt offerings."

They Have Forgotten Their Maker

Hosea 8:14

"For Israel has forgotten his Maker and built palaces, and Judah has multiplied fortified cities; so I will send a fire upon his cities, and it shall devour her strongholds."

Out of Egypt I Call My Son

Hosea 11:1-3 (KJV)

"When Israel was a child, then I loved him, and called My son out of Egypt. As they called them, so they went from them: they sacrificed unto Baalim, and burned incense to graven images. I taught Ephraim also to go, taking them by their arms; but they knew not that I healed them."

Hosea 11:4-5

"I led them with cords of kindness, with the bands of love, and I became to them as one who eases the yoke on their jaws, and I bent down to them and fed them.

They shall not return to the land of Egypt, but Assyria shall be their king, because they have refused to return to Me."

"Besides Me There Is No Savior"

Hosea 13:4-6

"But I am the LORD your God from the land of Egypt; you know no God but Me, and besides Me there is no Savior. It was I who knew you in the wilderness, in the land of drought; but when they had grazed, they became full, they were filled, and their heart was lifted up; therefore they forgot Me."

"I Shall Save Them From Death" (A Promise of Eternal Life to Be Fulfilled by Jesus)

Hosea 13:14 (GW)

"I want to free them from the power of the grave. I want to reclaim them from death. Death, I want to be a plague to you. Grave, I want to destroy you. I won't even think of changing My plans."

"I Shall Heal Their Backsliding (Abandoning of My Principles)"

Hosea 14:4-9 (KJV)
> "I will heal their backsliding, I will love them freely: for Mine anger is turned away from him.
>
> I will be as the dew unto Israel: he shall grow as the lily, and cast forth his roots as Lebanon.
>
> His branches shall spread, and his beauty shall be as the olive tree, and his smell as Lebanon. They that dwell under his shadow shall return; they shall revive as the corn, and grow as the vine: the scent thereof shall be as the wine of Lebanon.
>
> Ephraim shall say, What have I to do any more with idols? I have heard him, and observed him: I am like a green fir tree. From Me is thy fruit found.
>
> Who is wise, and he shall understand these things? prudent, and he shall know them? For the ways of the LORD are right, and the just shall walk in them: but the transgressors shall fall therein."

 ## Glory to Glory Q&A

1. Have you ever been betrayed in a relationship by a spouse, a friend or a loved one?
   If so, how did you feel? What was your reaction?
2. Describe a time when you felt intimately close to the Lord.

Chapter 8

Prophets Isaiah and Micah

God Declares an "End" and a "New Thing" Through Prophet Isaiah (760 - 673 BC)

There are many theologians who will be able to answer your many questions about the structure and theology of the book of Isaiah. I am not one of them.

Isaiah lived during the same time as the Kings Uzziah, Jotham, Ahaz, and Hezekiah, the tenth to thirteenth kings of Judah. At the time, Judah was threatened by their neighbor, Assyria (Isaiah 1).

One Night

Remember Esther?

She did anything to please the king. Then the king invited her to spend one night with him, as he did with all the girls in the harem.

But Esther was different. I imagine that King Ahashuerus talked to her about things he never shared with anyone else. I bet they shared a few intimate moments where he shared with her what he liked and what he didn't like. Maybe he even told her the plans and dreams he had for the future of his kingdom.

For these are the kind of things that a bridegroom would share with the woman that he was about to choose to be his bride.

Bride of Christ, this is your night with the king.

God is revealing His heart to you. He is sharing His most intimate thoughts and dreams. He shares with you the things that cause His anguish and pain. You are privileged to be taken into the king's chamber where you may listen to His voice.

This chapter and the next are your one night with the king. Even though He is talking through the prophets, He is speaking directly with you. How often have you longed to hear His voice? How many nights and days have you searched to know Him - to know what He is like, to know Him more intimately?

Well, this is your moment to hear from Him directly.

Imagine that you are sitting with Him as He speaks with you face-to-face. Perhaps you could even see a glimmer of tears in His eyes as He speaks softly so that only you can hear.

The Lord's Sorrow

My Children Forgot Who They Were

"Children have I raised and brought up, but they have rebelled against Me.

The ox knows its owner, and the donkey its master's crib; but Israel does not understand, My people do not know. They have forgotten Me.

They have become evildoers, children who deal corruptly" (Isaiah 1:2-4).

They Were Worshipping Anything But God

"The house of Jacob is full of things from the east, fortune telling, and idols.

They have many riches – silver, gold, chariots, horses, and many treasures. They are bowing down to idols that they made with their own hands instead of worshipping Me, their God" (Isaiah 2:6-8).

Puffed Up With Pride

"Their pride and idolatry are why I, the Lord, humbled them. Their haughty looks and lofty pride need to be humbled and I, the Lord alone, shall be praised. That is why they were sent into exile – for their lack of knowledge of Me, their Lord. They refused to learn what pleases Me.

I, the Lord, have a day against all that is proud and lifted up – it shall be brought low" (Isaiah 2:9-22, 5:13).

His Vineyard

Isaiah 5:1-2&4-7 (GW)
> Let me sing a love song to my Beloved about His vineyard: My Beloved had a vineyard on a fertile hill.
>
> He dug it up, removed its stones, planted it with the choicest vines, built a watchtower in it, and made a winepress in it. Then He waited for it to produce good grapes, but it produced only sour, wild grapes.
>
> What more could have been done for My vineyard than what I have already done for it? When I waited for it to produce good grapes, why did it produce only sour, wild grapes?
>
> Now then, let Me tell you what I will do to My vineyard. I will tear away its hedge so that it can be devoured and tear down its wall so that it can be trampled.
>
> I will make it a wasteland. It will never be pruned or hoed. Thorns and weeds will grow in it, and I will command the clouds not to rain on it.
>
> The vineyard of the LORD of Armies is the nation of Israel, and the people of Judah are the garden of His delight. He hoped for justice but saw only slaughter, for righteousness but heard only cries of distress.

They Serve Me With Their Lips, but Their Hearts Are Far From Me

Isaiah 29:13-14
> And the Lord said: "Because this people draw near with their mouth and honor Me with their lips, while their hearts are far from Me, and their fear of Me is a commandment taught by men, therefore, behold, I will again do wonderful things with this people, with wonder upon wonder; and the wisdom of their wise men shall perish, and the discernment of their discerning men shall be hidden."

They Were Doing Things in Secret and Thought That It Would Not Be Noticed by Their Maker

Isaiah 29:15-16
> Ah, you who hide deep from the LORD your counsel, whose deeds are in the dark, and who say, "Who sees us? Who knows us?" You turn things upside down! Shall the potter be regarded as the clay, that the thing made should say of its maker, "He did not make me"; or the thing formed say of him who formed it, "He has no understanding"?

"They Carried Out a Plan, but Not Mine"

Isaiah 30:1
> "Ah, stubborn children," declares the LORD, "who carry out a plan, but not Mine, and who make an alliance, but not of My Spirit, that they may add sin to sin"

Isaiah 30:8-11
> "And now, go, write it before them on a tablet and inscribe it in a book, that it may be for the time to come as a witness forever. For they are a rebellious people, lying children, children unwilling to hear the instruction of the LORD; who say to the seers, 'Do not see,' and to the prophets, 'Do not prophesy to us what is right; speak to us smooth things, prophesy illusions, leave the way, turn aside from the path, let us hear no more about the Holy One of Israel.'"

Their Wrongdoings Caused a Separation Between Them and God

Isaiah 59:1-3
> Behold, the LORD's hand is not shortened, that it cannot save, or His ear dull, that it cannot hear; but your iniquities have made a separation between you and your God, and your sins have hidden His face from you so that He does not hear. For your hands are defiled with blood and your fingers with iniquity; your lips have spoken lies; your tongue mutters wickedness.

They Grieved His Holy Spirit by Rebelling Against His Guidance

Isaiah 63:10-14
> But they rebelled and grieved His Holy Spirit; therefore He turned to be their enemy, and Himself fought against them. Then He remembered the days of old, of Moses and his people. Where is He who brought them up out of the sea with the shepherds of His flock?

> Where is He who put in the midst of them His Holy Spirit, who caused His glorious arm to go at the right hand of Moses, who divided the waters before them to make for Himself an everlasting name, who led them through the depths? Like a horse in the desert, they did not stumble.

> Like livestock that go down into the valley, the Spirit of the LORD gave them rest. So You led your people, to make for Yourself a glorious name.

The Holy Spirit led Israel continuously, but they continuously murmured, complained, and rebelled against the Lord. Many shrank back in fear of the giants in Canaan, unwilling to believe the Lord that He would give them the victory as promised.

They stubbornly refused to teach their children the ways of the Lord, as the Holy Spirit had told them to do. Because of their disobedience, generations to come suffered harm, for they didn't know the Lord.

They stubbornly rejected and ignored the Lord's presence by pursuing "help" from other useless gods, who were not gods at all.

The Lord Earnestly Reassures That He Is Trustworthy

By Providing Security for as He Planned, so Shall It Be

You can always rely on the Lord. If He promised something, it is rock solid. He will deliver on His promise.

Isaiah 14:24-27
> The LORD of hosts has sworn: "As I have planned, so shall it be, and as I have purposed, so shall it stand, that I will break the Assyrian in My land, and on My mountains trample him underfoot; and his yoke shall depart from them, and his burden from their shoulder."
>
> This is the purpose that is purposed concerning the whole earth, and this is the hand that is stretched out over all the nations. For the LORD of hosts has purposed, and who will annul it? His hand is stretched out, and who will turn it back?

He Provides Perfect Peace

Isaiah 26:3-4
> You keep him in perfect peace whose mind is stayed on You, because he trusts in You. Trust in the LORD forever, for the LORD GOD is an everlasting rock.

The Lord Will Be Gracious as Soon as He Hears Your Cry

The Lord is gracious and desires to show mercy to you. He lingers expectantly to hear you ask Him for help.

When you turn to the Lord for help (after realizing that only He can help you), you will also realize that He allowed you to make mistakes and take detours to teach you that only He can help you. You will hear a voice behind you saying, "This is the way, walk in it," like a guide leading a blind.

Then you will boldly say to anything else, "Be Gone!" for you learned to put your faith in God (read Isaiah 30:18-22).

All Flesh is Grass, but the Word of God Stands Forever

Isaiah 40:6-8

> A voice says, "Cry!" And I said, "What shall I cry?" All flesh is grass, and all its beauty is like the flower of the field. The grass withers, the flower fades when the breath of the LORD blows on it; surely the people are grass. The grass withers, the flower fades, but <u>the word of our God will stand forever</u> (see also 1 Peter 1:24).

Have You Not Heard?

Isaiah 40:28-31

> Have you not known? Have you not heard? The LORD is the everlasting God, the Creator of the ends of the earth. He does not faint or grow weary; His understanding is unsearchable.
>
> He gives power to the faint, and to him who has no might He increases strength. Even youths shall faint and be weary, and young men shall fall exhausted; but they who wait for the LORD shall renew their strength; they shall mount up with wings like eagles; they shall run and not be weary; they shall walk and not faint.

"I Called the Generations From the Beginning"

Isaiah 41:4

> "Who has performed and done this, calling the generations from the beginning? I, the LORD, the first, and with the last; I am He."

The Lord has chosen you, the offspring of Abraham, whom He called from the farthest corners of the earth saying, "Fear not, for I am with you. Do not be alarmed, for I am your God. Those who are at war with you will be dealt with. I will strengthen you and uphold you with My righteous right hand. I am the one who helps you" (paraphrased from Isaiah 41:8-13).

"When There is No Water for the Poor and Needy"

Isaiah 41:17-20:

> "When the poor and needy seek water, and there is none, and their tongue is parched with thirst, I the LORD will answer them; I the God of Israel will not forsake them.
>
> I will open rivers on the bare heights, and fountains in the midst of the valleys. I will make the wilderness a pool of water, and the dry land springs of water. I will put in the wilderness the cedar, the acacia, the myrtle, and the olive.

I will set in the desert the cypress, the plane and the pine together, that they may **see** and **know**, may consider and understand together, that the hand of the LORD has done this, the Holy One of Israel has created it."

"Besides Me There Is No God"

Isaiah 44:6-8 (GW)
> The LORD is Israel's King and defender. He is the LORD of Armies. This is what the LORD says: "I am the first and the last, and there is no God except Me.
>
> If there is anyone like Me, let him say so. Let him tell Me what happened when I established My people long ago. Then let him predict what will happen to them.
>
> Don't be terrified or afraid. Didn't I make this known to you long ago? You are My witnesses. Is there any God except Me? There is no other rock; I know of none."

"Do Not Fear What They Fear"

The Lord spoke to Isaiah saying, "Do not walk in the way of this people or fear what they fear, but honor the Lord as holy" (Isaiah 8:11-3).

The Silliness of Idolatry, When GOD is Creator of Everything

Everyone who makes themselves idols is silly. Those things they delight in have no profit at all. Who shapes a god or makes an image of an idol that is profitable for nothing? They will be embarrassed by their ignorance (Isaiah 44:9-17).

It is silly to make gods out of things that God Himself made. It is much better to worship your Maker than to worship anything that He made.

That You May KNOW Him Who Calls You

Isaiah 45:2-3 (ISV)
> "I Myself will go before you, and He will make the mountains level; I'll shatter bronze doors and cut through iron bars.
>
> I'll give you concealed treasures and riches hidden in secret places, so that you'll know that it is I, the LORD, the God of Israel, who calls you by name."

Declaring Things Before They Happen, so That He Is Proven Truthful, All-knowing and Trustworthy

Isaiah 48:3-5
> "The former things I declared of old; they went out from My mouth, and I announced them; then suddenly I did them, and they came to pass. Because I know that you are obstinate, and your neck is an iron sinew and your forehead brass, I declared them to you from of old, before they came to pass I announced them to you, lest you should say, 'My idol did them, my carved image and my metal image commanded them.'"

"I Bring My Righteousness and My Salvation"

God gives hope to those who struggle to do things right.

God's hope is that from ancient times, before there was anything, He purposed to bring about His righteousness and His salvation as the solution to help all who cry out for help.

Isaiah 46:8-13
> "Remember this and stand firm, recall it to mind, you transgressors, remember the former things of old; for I am God, and there is no other; I am God, and there is none like Me, declaring the end from the beginning and from ancient times things not yet done, saying, 'My counsel shall stand, and I will accomplish all My purpose,' calling a bird of prey from the east, the man of My counsel from a far country. I have spoken, and I will bring it to pass; I have purposed, and I will do it.
>
> Listen to Me, you stubborn of heart, you who are far from righteousness: I bring near My righteousness; it is not far off, and My salvation will not delay; I will put salvation in Zion, for Israel My glory."

The Lord Cannot Forget You

Isaiah 49:14-16
> But Zion said, "The LORD has forsaken me; my Lord has forgotten me."
>
> "Can a woman forget her nursing child, that she should have no compassion on the son of her womb? Even these may forget, yet I will not forget you. Behold, I have engraved you on the palms of My hands; your walls are continually before Me."

"I Live With the Broken"

"I live in a high and holy place and also with those of a crushed and wounded spirit. Those who are free from self-assertive pride and look to Me for help, I will restore back to life. I will revive the heart of those who feel true sorrow when they realize that they have done something wrong." (Isaiah 57:13-15)

The Lord's Promise: His Spirit and Words Will Never Leave You

Isaiah 59:21
"And as for Me, this is My covenant with them," says the LORD: "My Spirit that is upon you, and My words that I have put in your mouth, shall not depart out of your mouth, or out of the mouth of your offspring, or out of the mouth of your children's offspring," says the LORD, "from this time forth and forevermore."

The Messiah

The Lord releases what the Messiah will look like and what He will do.

Immanuel

A virgin will conceive and bear a son, and call Him Immanuel, which means "God with us".

He will know how to refuse evil and choose well (Isaiah 7:14-15).

A Sanctuary and a Rock of Stumbling

He will become a sanctuary and a rock of offense and stumbling as He confronts and breaks open their secrets, to heal them (Isaiah 8:14-15).

Those in Anguish and Darkness

There was gloom and anguish in the land of Zebulun and Naphtali, the land beyond the Jordan, Galilee of the nations. The people who walked in darkness will see a great light to show them the way (Isaiah 9:1-2; fulfilled in Matthew 4:15-16).

For to Us a Child Is Born, With Government on His Shoulder! (Acts 15:16-17)

Isaiah 9:6-7 (KJV)
"For unto us a child is born, unto us a Son is given: and the government shall be upon his shoulder: and His name shall be called Wonderful, Counsellor, The mighty God, The everlasting Father, and The Prince of Peace.

Of the increase of His government and peace there shall be no end, upon the throne of David, and upon his kingdom, to order it, and to establish it with judgment and with justice from henceforth even forever. The zeal of the LORD of hosts will perform this.

The Branch From the Root of Jesse (the Father of David, the Bloodline of Jesus)

Isaiah 11:1-10
>There shall come forth a shoot from the stump of Jesse, and a branch from his roots shall bear fruit. And <u>the Spirit of the LORD shall rest upon Him</u>, the <u>Spirit of wisdom</u> and <u>understanding</u>, the Spirit of <u>counsel</u> and <u>might</u>, the Spirit of <u>knowledge</u> and <u>the fear of the LORD</u>.
>
>And His delight shall be in the fear of the LORD. He shall not judge by what His eyes see, or decide disputes by what His ears hear, but with righteousness He shall judge the <u>poor</u>, and decide with equity for the <u>meek</u> of the earth; and He shall strike the earth with the rod of His mouth, and with the breath of His lips He shall destroy the wicked.
>
><u>Righteousness</u> shall be the belt of His waist, and <u>faithfulness</u> the belt of His loins. The wolf shall dwell with the lamb, and the leopard shall lie down with the young goat, and the calf and the lion and the fattened calf together; and a little child shall lead them.
>
>The cow and the bear shall graze; their young shall lie down together; and the lion shall eat straw like the ox. The nursing child shall play over the hole of the cobra, and the weaned child shall put his hand on the adder's den. They shall not hurt or destroy in all My holy mountain; for the earth shall be full of the knowledge of the LORD as the waters cover the sea.
>
>In that day the root of Jesse, He shall stand as a signal for the peoples – of Him shall the nations inquire, and His resting place shall be glorious.

The Lord Is My Strength and My Song, My Salvation

Isaiah 12:1-2
>You will say in that day: "I will give thanks to you, O LORD, for though You were angry with me, Your anger turned away, that You might comfort me. "Behold, God is my salvation; I will trust, and will not be afraid; for the LORD GOD is my strength and my song, and He has become my salvation."

You Will Draw Water From the Wells of Salvation

Isaiah 12:3-6
>With joy you will draw water from the wells of salvation. And you will say in that day: "Give thanks to the LORD, call upon His name, make known His deeds among the peoples, proclaim that His name is exalted.

"Sing praises to the LORD, for He has done gloriously; let this be made known in all the earth. Shout, and sing for joy, O inhabitant of Zion, for great in your midst is the Holy One of Israel."

He Will be Savior to the Poor and Needy, Remove the Veil, and Swallow up Death Forever!

Isaiah 25:4-9

For You have been a stronghold to the <u>poor</u>, a stronghold to the <u>needy</u> in his distress, a <u>shelter</u> from the storm and a <u>shade</u> from the heat; for the breath of the ruthless is like a storm against a wall, like heat in a dry place. You subdue the noise of the foreigners; as heat by the shade of a cloud, so the song of the ruthless is put down.

On this mountain the LORD of hosts will make <u>for all peoples</u> a feast of rich food, a feast of well-aged wine, of rich food full of marrow, of aged wine well refined.

And He will swallow up on this mountain the covering that is cast over all peoples, the veil that is spread over all nations. He will swallow up death forever; and the Lord GOD will wipe away tears from all faces, and the reproach of His people He will take away from all the earth, for the LORD has spoken.

It will be said on that day, "Behold, this is our God; we have waited for Him, that He might save us. This is the LORD; we have waited for Him; let us be glad and rejoice in His salvation."

A Cornerstone in Zion – Whoever Believes in Him Will Not Worry

Isaiah 28:16 (GW)

This is what the Almighty LORD says: I am going to lay a rock in Zion, a rock that has been tested, a precious cornerstone, a solid foundation. Whoever believes in him will not worry.

When the Spirit Is Poured Out From on High

Isaiah 32:14-15

For the palace is forsaken, the populous city deserted; the hill and the watchtower will become dens forever, a joy of wild donkeys, a pasture of flocks; until the Spirit is poured upon us from on high, and the wilderness becomes a fruitful field, and the fruitful field is deemed a forest.

The Fruit of His Righteousness Will Be Eternal Peace, Quietness and Trust

Isaiah 32:16-18

"Then justice will dwell in the wilderness, and righteousness abide in the fruitful field. And the effect of righteousness will be peace, and the result of righteousness, quietness and trust forever.

My people will abide in a peaceful habitation, in secure dwellings, and in quiet resting places."

The Glory of the Lord, to Be Revealed in Christ, the Messiah – Deaf Shall Hear and Blind Shall See!

Isaiah 35:3-10

Strengthen the weak hands, and make firm the feeble knees. Say to those who have an anxious heart, "Be strong; fear not! Behold, your God will come with vengeance, with the recompense of God. He will come and save you."

Then the eyes of the blind shall be opened, and the ears of the deaf unstopped; then shall the lame man leap like a deer, and the tongue of the mute sing for joy (also Isaiah 29:18-19). For waters break forth in the wilderness, and streams in the desert; the burning sand shall become a pool, and the thirsty ground springs of water; in the haunt of jackals, where they lie down, the grass shall become reeds and rushes.

And a highway shall be there, and it shall be called the Way of Holiness; the unclean shall not pass over it. It shall belong to those who walk on the way; even if they are fools, they shall not go astray. No lion shall be there, nor shall any ravenous beast come up on it; they shall not be found there, but the redeemed shall walk there. And the ransomed of the LORD shall return and come to Zion with singing; everlasting joy shall be upon their heads; they shall obtain gladness and joy, and sorrow and sighing shall flee away.

Comfort for God's People- Preparing the Way for the Lord's Glory!

Isaiah 40:1-5

Comfort, comfort My people, says your God. Speak tenderly to Jerusalem, and cry to her that her warfare is ended, that her iniquity is pardoned, that she has received from the LORD's hand double for all her sins.

A voice cries: "In the wilderness prepare the way of the LORD; make straight in the desert a highway for our God. Every valley shall be lifted up, and every mountain and hill be made low; the uneven ground shall become level, and the rough places a plain. And the glory of the LORD shall be revealed, and all flesh shall see it together, for the mouth of the LORD has spoken."

John the Baptist was the voice in the wilderness that prepared the way for Jesus, God's Son, to come and save the world from their sins.

He Will Tend His Flock Like a Shepherd

The Messiah will tend His flock like a shepherd and carry the lambs in His arms. He will gently lead those who are with the young (Isaiah 40:10-11, John 10).

The Lord's Chosen Servant – The Messiah (Matthew 12:18-21) - The New Things Declared!

Isaiah 42:1-9
> Behold My Servant, whom I uphold, My chosen, in whom My soul delights; I have put My Spirit upon Him; He will bring forth justice to the nations. He will not cry aloud or lift up His voice, or make it heard in the street; a bruised reed He will not break, and a faintly burning wick He will not quench; He will faithfully bring forth justice.
>
> He will not grow faint or be discouraged till He has established justice in the earth; and the coastlands wait for His law.
>
> Thus says God, the LORD, who created the heavens and stretched them out, who spread out the earth and what comes from it, who gives breath to the people on it and spirit to those who walk in it:
>
> "I am the LORD; I have called you in righteousness; I will take you by the hand and keep you; I will give you as a covenant for the people, a light for the nations, to open the eyes that are blind, to bring out the prisoners from the dungeon, from the prison those who sit in darkness. I am the LORD; that is My name; My glory I give to no other, nor My praise to carved idols.
>
> Behold, the former things have come to pass, and **new** things I now declare; before they spring forth I tell you of them."

Every Knee Shall Bow and Every Tongue Confess That He Is God

Isaiah 45:22-23
> "Turn to Me and be saved, all the ends of the earth! For I am God, and there is no other.

By Myself I have sworn; from My mouth has gone out in righteousness a word that shall not return: 'To Me every knee shall bow, every tongue shall swear allegiance.'"

Only in the Lord Are Righteousness and Strength

Isaiah 45:24-25
"Only in the LORD, it shall be said of Me, are righteousness and strength; to Him shall come and be ashamed all who were incensed against Him. In the LORD all the offspring of Israel shall be justified and shall glory."

Isaiah 45:7-8
"I form light and create darkness; I make well-being and create calamity; I am the LORD, who does all these things. Shower, O heavens, from above, and let the clouds rain down righteousness; let the earth open, that salvation and righteousness may bear fruit; let the earth cause them both to sprout; I the LORD have created it." (See also Isaiah 51:3-8)

Isaiah 61:11
For as the earth brings forth its sprouts, and as a garden causes what is sown in it to sprout up, so the Lord GOD will cause righteousness and praise to sprout up before all the nations.

The Servant of the Lord – A Light for the Nations, Salvation to the Ends of the Earth!

Isaiah 49:6
"It is too light a thing that you should be My servant to raise up the tribes of Jacob and to bring back the preserved of Israel; I will make you as a light for the nations, that My salvation may reach to the end of the earth."

He Will Follow Father God's Lead

Isaiah 50:4-5
"The Lord GOD has given Me the tongue of those who are taught, that I may know how to sustain with a word him who is weary. Morning by morning He awakens; He awakens My ear to hear as those who are taught. The Lord GOD has opened My ear, and I was not rebellious; I turned not backward."

He Will Be Beaten, but Remain Steadfast

Isaiah 50:6-7
"I gave My back to those who strike, and My cheeks to those who pull out the beard; I hid not My face from disgrace and spitting. But the Lord

GOD helps Me; therefore I have not been disgraced; therefore I have set My face like a flint, and I know that I shall not be put to shame."

God's Victory Over Sin Decreed

Despised and Pierced for Your Mistakes, Griefs and Pains

The Lord's Servant will be wise and lifted up. He will be marred beyond human resemblance to save many nations (paraphrased from Isaiah 52:13-15).

He was despised and rejected by men, a man of sorrows, familiar with grief.

All your griefs and pains were laid upon Him, and He carried all your sorrows. He was pierced for your transgressions, mistakes, perversions, and shortcomings. He was crushed for your iniquities and took the punishment for sins to establish peace with God. Thereby, He removed the separation between man and God, the division caused by sin, to bring about Godly reconciliation.

By His wounds, you are healed.

Through it all, He remained silent, like a lamb led to the slaughter. His grave was with the wicked and with a rich man in His death, although He had done no violence, and there was no deceit in His mouth (paraphrased from Isaiah 53:1-9).

Isaiah 59:15-16
> Truth is lacking, and he who departs from evil makes himself a prey. The LORD saw it, and it displeased Him that there was no justice. He saw that there was no man, and wondered that there was no one to intercede; then His own arm brought him salvation, and His righteousness upheld him.

He Will Bind up the Broken-hearted and Set the Captives Free, so They Can Be Restored and Experience Blessing

Isaiah 61:1-3 (ISV)
> "The Spirit of the LORD is upon Me, because the LORD has anointed Me; He has sent me to bring good news to the oppressed and to bind up the brokenhearted, to proclaim freedom for the captives, and release from darkness for the prisoners; to proclaim the year of the LORD's favor, the day of vengeance of our God; to comfort all who mourn;
>
> to provide for those who grieve in Zion – to bestow on them a crown of beauty instead of ashes, the oil of gladness instead of mourning, a mantle of praise instead of a spirit of despair."

"Then people will call them "Oaks of Righteousness", "'The Planting of the LORD", in order to display his splendor."

Because He has healed the broken, they will be empowered to rebuild the ruins of their lives and to restore places that have been deserted for far too many generations.

They will be called servants of God and instead of their shame, they will receive a double portion in their land. Everlasting joy will be theirs, for the Lord loves justice and hates stealing and wrongdoing. He will faithfully reward you and make an everlasting agreement with you.

Your children will be known among the nations. All who see them will know that they are children of God and will acknowledge that He has blessed them (Isaiah 61:6-9).

Then you will greatly rejoice in the Lord! Your soul will praise God and lift His Name up high, because He has covered your guilt and inadequacies with the garments of salvation.

He covered your shame with the robe of righteousness, as a bridegroom takes care in dressing himself for his wedding day, and as a bride shows great attention to detail in adorning herself with jewels and decorations that are precious to her (Isaiah 61:10).

Your Scarlet Sins Shall Become Like Snow

God was planning to deal once and for all with the separation between Him and people – a separation caused by their sins, so that He can help them to overcome their flesh and live blessed lives, for the glory of His name.

Isaiah 1:18 (KJV)
"Come now, and let us reason together," saith the LORD: "though your sins be as scarlet, they shall be as white as snow; though they be red like crimson, they shall be as wool."

Isaiah 43:25-28
"I, I am He who blots out your transgressions for My own sake, and I will not remember your sins. Put Me in remembrance; let us argue together; set forth your case, that you may be proved right. Your first father sinned, and your mediators transgressed against Me. Therefore I will profane the princes of the sanctuary, and deliver Jacob to utter destruction and Israel to reviling."

The Lord Will Make a Full End

Isaiah 10:20-23
In that day the remnant of Israel and the survivors of the house of Jacob will no more lean on him (the Assyrians) who struck them, but will lean

on the LORD, the Holy One of Israel, in truth. A remnant will return, the remnant of Jacob, to the mighty God. For though your people Israel be as the sand of the sea, only a remnant of them will return. Destruction is decreed, overflowing with righteousness.

For the Lord GOD of hosts will make a full end, as decreed, in the midst of all the earth.

The Yoke of Oppression Will Be Broken by the Anointing

The Lord promised to deliver His people, who live in Zion, and for them not to be afraid of their oppressors. He reassured Judah and Israel that His fury about their rejection of Him and all their idols and abominations will come to an end. He will deliver them from the Assyrians as He delivered them from the Egyptians when Moses raised his staff. The burden will depart from them because of the fat, His anointing (Isaiah 10:24-27).

Man Will Again Look to His Maker, Whom They Had Forgotten, and Not to the Idols Made by His Own Hand

Isaiah 17:7-11

In that day man will look to his Maker, and his eyes will look on the Holy One of Israel.

He will not look to the altars, the work of his hands, and he will not look on what his own fingers have made, either the Asherim or the altars of incense. In that day their strong cities will be like the deserted places of the wooded heights and the hilltops, which they deserted because of the children of Israel, and there will be desolation.

For you have forgotten the God of your salvation and have not remembered the Rock of your refuge; therefore, though you plant pleasant plants and sow the vine-branch of a stranger, though you make them grow on the day that you plant them, and make them blossom in the morning that you sow, yet the harvest will flee away in a day of grief and incurable pain.

Those Who Go Astray in Spirit Will Come to Understanding

Concerning the house of Jacob, the Lord who rescued Abraham promised that Jacob will no longer be ashamed. When he sees his children, and what the Lord has done in them, his face will no longer grow pale.

The children will sanctify the Lord's name and recognize His name as holy. They will stand in awe of God. Those who go astray in spirit will come to understanding and those who complain will accept instruction (Isaiah 29:22-24).

"Fear Not! Bring My Sons and My Daughters – Everyone Who Is Called by My Name!"

Isaiah 43:1-7
>But now thus says the LORD, He who created you, O Jacob, He who formed you, O Israel: "Fear not, for I have redeemed you; I have called you by name, you are Mine.
>
>When you pass through the waters, I will be with you; and through the rivers, they shall not overwhelm you; when you walk through fire you shall not be burned, and the flame shall not consume you.
>
>For I am the LORD your God, the Holy One of Israel, your Savior. I give Egypt as your ransom, Cush and Seba in exchange for you. Because you are precious in My eyes, and honored, and I love you, I give men in return for you, peoples in exchange for your life.
>
>Fear not, for I am with you; I will bring your offspring from the east, and from the west I will gather you.
>
>I will say to the north, Give up, and to the south, Do not withhold; bring My sons from afar and My daughters from the end of the earth, everyone who is called by My name, whom I created for My glory, whom I formed and made."

"Assemble All Peoples That They May Know I Alone Am Your Savior!"

Isaiah 43:8-13
>Bring out the people who are blind, yet have eyes, who are deaf, yet have ears!
>
>All the nations gather together, and the peoples assemble. Who among them can declare this, and show us the former things? Let them bring their witnesses to prove them right, and let them hear and say, 'It is true'.
>
>"You are My witnesses," declares the LORD, "and My Servant whom I have chosen, that you may **know** and **believe** Me and understand that I am He. Before Me no god was formed, nor shall there be any after Me.
>
>I, I am the LORD, and besides Me there is no savior. I declared and saved and proclaimed, when there was no strange god among you; and you are My witnesses," declares the LORD, "and I am God. Also henceforth I am He; there is none who can deliver from My hand; I work, and who can turn it back?"

The Lord Is Doing a New Thing, Things That Were Hidden!

Isaiah 43:19 (KJV)
> Behold, I will do a new thing; now it shall spring forth; shall ye not know it? I will even make a way in the wilderness, and rivers in the desert.

Isaiah 48:6-11 (GW)
> You've heard these words. Now look at all this. Won't you admit it? From now on I will reveal to you new things, hidden things that you do not know. They are created now, not in the past. You haven't heard about them before today, so you can't say that you already knew about them.
>
> You have never heard about them. You have never known about them. Your ears have never been open to hear them before. I know that you've acted very treacherously and that you have been called a rebel since you were born.
>
> For My name's sake I'll be patient. For My glory's sake I'll hold My anger back from you, rather than destroy you.
>
> I have refined you, but not like silver. I have tested you in the furnace of suffering.
>
> I am doing this for Myself, only for Myself. Why should My name be dishonored? I will not give My glory to anyone else.

I Will Pour Out My Spirit Upon Jacob's Offspring

God promises to pour out His Spirit on His servant Israel whom He chose. He will pour waters on a thirsty land and streams on dry ground. He will pour out His blessings on Israel's children and they will be like willows by flowing streams (Isaiah 44:1-4).

Isaiah 44:5
> This one will say, 'I am the LORD's,' another will call on the name of Jacob, and another will write on his hand, 'The LORD's,' and name himself by the name of Israel."

The Eternal Covenant of Peace – The Barren, the Gentiles, to Become Betrothed to God!

"Sing, O barren one (the Gentiles), for the children of the desolate one will be more than the children of her who is married," says the LORD (Isaiah 54).
"Prepare for expansion and blessing!

You will spread abroad to the right and to the left, and your children will possess the nations and will populate the lost cities.

Do not be afraid! You will not be ashamed. You will forget your humiliation and the embarrassment of your hopelessness you will remember no more.

For your Maker is your Husband, the Lord of hosts is His name. The holy one of Israel is your Redeemer, the God of the whole earth He is called.

With everlasting love, the Lord will cherish you. He will be your Redeemer, the one who rescues, justifies, and compensates for your weaknesses.

All your children will be taught by the Lord. Their peace shall be exceedingly great. You will be far from oppression, and you need not be afraid. In righteousness, you will be established. If anyone stirs up strife, it is not from me, and they will stumble over their own schemes. No weapon that is formed against you shall prosper.

This is the inheritance of God's children. Their vindication, meaning the action of clearing their name of blame or suspicion, and proof that someone is in right standing and justified are from the Lord."

Isaiah 56:8
> The Lord GOD, who gathers the outcasts of Israel, declares, "I will gather yet others (the Gentiles) to Him besides those already gathered."

Isaiah 65:1
> "I was ready to be sought by those (the Gentiles) who did not ask for Me; I was ready to be found by those who did not seek Me. I said, 'Here I am, here I am,' to a nation that was not called by My name."

Calling ALL Who Are Thirsty, the Lord Will Be Found by All Who Seek Him

"Come, everyone who is thirsty! Come to the fountain of living waters. Buy the wine of salvation and the milk of the Word without money and without price (Isaiah 55).

Why do you spend your money on something that cannot feed you? Why do you labor for things that cannot fulfill you?

The Lord invites you to listen carefully to Him and feed on Him, that you may live.

He makes an everlasting agreement, as He did with David, to call a nation that you do not know (the Gentiles), and they will run to the Lord.

Seek the Lord while He may be found. Seek His help while He is close to you. Let those who lie, cheat, and plan harm turn away from their loveless behavior and thoughts. Rather return to the Lord that He may have compassion with you, for He pardons abundantly and is very understanding when you ask Him for help.

Every word that has gone out from His mouth shall not return to Him empty, but it shall succeed in its purpose. This is as certain as rain waters the earth to make things grow, producing both seed to the sower as well as food to the eater – supplying a solution, according to their needs.

God's ways are higher than your ways and His thoughts are higher than your thoughts.

You will experience joy and be led in peace. The hurtful thorn will be replaced by the soft cypress, and a prickly shrub will be replaced by an evergreen shrub that smells lovely and has beautiful flowers. These beautiful trees will bring praises and glory to the Name of the Lord.

New Heavens and a New Earth

Isaiah 65:17-18
"For behold, I create new heavens and a new earth, and the former things shall not be remembered or come into mind. But be glad and rejoice forever in that which I create; for behold, I create Jerusalem to be a joy, and her people to be a gladness."

Isaiah 65:19-25 (ISV)
"I'll rejoice over Jerusalem, and take delight in My people; no longer will the sound of weeping be heard in it, nor the cry of distress.

And there will no longer be in it a young boy who lives only a few days, or an old person who does not live out his days; for one who dies at a hundred years will be thought a mere youth, and one who falls short of a hundred years will be considered accursed.

People will build houses and live in them; They'll plant vineyards and eat their fruit.

They won't build for others to inhabit; they won't plant for others to eat – for like the lifetime of a tree, so will the lifetime of My people be, and My chosen ones will long enjoy the work of their hands.

They won't toil in vain nor bear children doomed to misfortune, for they will be offspring blessed by the LORD, they and their descendants with them.

Before they call, I will answer, while they are still speaking, I'll hear.

The wolf and the lamb will feed together, and the lion will eat straw like the ox; but as for the serpent – its food will be dust! They won't harm or destroy on My entire holy mountain," says the LORD.

Other Guidance From the Lord

Earnest Warning to Not Exalt Yourself Like Lucifer Did

There is only one God, Maker of everything.

The work of the Maker is not greater than the Maker.

When God allows you to be a city on a hill, it is to bring honor, praises and glory to Him alone!

Isaiah 14:12 (KJV)
> How art thou fallen from heaven, O Lucifer, son of the morning! How art thou cut down to the ground, which didst weaken the nations!

Isaiah 14:13-17 (ISV)
> You said in your heart, 'I'll ascend to heaven, above the stars of God. I'll erect my throne; I'll sit on the Mount of Assembly in the far reaches of the north; I'll ascend above the tops of the clouds; I'll make myself like the Most High.'
>
> But you are brought down to join the dead, to the far reaches of the Pit.
>
> Those who see you will stare at you. They will wonder about you: 'Is this the man who made the earth tremble, who made kingdoms quake, who made the world like a desert, who destroyed its cities, who would not open the jails for his prisoners?'

Jesus said that He saw satan fall like lighting from heaven (Luke 10:18). John confirmed that the dragon, the ancient serpent, called the devil and satan, who deceives the whole world, was thrown down to earth, and his angels with him (Revelation 12:1-17).

Lucifer was created by God, and he was called the morning star. Then he wanted to lift himself high above God, so that he could be worshipped. That's just stupid.

God's glory is magnificent, but it's God's glory. When Moses met the Lord face-to-face, the people couldn't look at his face, for it shone greatly and Moses had to cover it (2 Corinthians 3:7-18). The difference between Moses and Lucifer is that Moses knew that it was God's glory, not his.

In this regard, be like Moses.

In Returning and Rest You Shall Be Saved

Isaiah 30:15
> For thus said the Lord GOD, the Holy One of Israel, "In returning and rest you shall be saved; in quietness and in trust shall be your strength."

The Lord's Invitation

Isaiah 44:22 (GW)
> I made your rebellious acts disappear like a thick cloud and your sins like the morning mist. Come back to Me, because I have reclaimed you.

Pay Attention to the Lord, and You Will See Blessing!

The Lord told Israel that He was the one who taught them to profit and led them in the way they should go.

If they had paid attention to His instructions, then their peace would have been like a river and their righteousness like the waves of the sea. Their children would have been like the sand and their name would never be cut off or destroyed before the Lord (Isaiah 48:17-19).

True Fasting Is to Free the Oppressed, Then You Will Be Satisfied

Pursue true fasting, which is to free the oppressed and to break every yoke. It is to share your bread with the hungry and your home with the homeless. It is to clothe those who are naked and to help your own relatives (Isaiah 58:6-7).

Isaiah 58:8-12
> Then shall your light break forth like the dawn, and your healing shall spring up speedily; your righteousness shall go before you; the glory of the LORD shall be your rear guard. Then you shall call, and the LORD will answer; you shall cry, and He will say, 'Here I am.'
>
> If you take away the yoke from your midst, the pointing of the finger, and speaking wickedness, if you pour yourself out for the hungry and satisfy the desire of the afflicted, then shall your light rise in the darkness and your gloom be as the noonday.
>
> And the LORD will guide you continually and satisfy your desire in scorched places and make your bones strong; and you shall be like a watered garden, like a spring of water, whose waters do not fail. And your ancient ruins shall be rebuilt; you shall raise up the foundations of many generations; you shall be called the repairer of the breach, the restorer of streets to dwell in.

God's Plan

Peace and Salvation to the Ends of the Earth

The Lord wants all the ends of the earth to see His salvation (Isaiah 52:7-10).

God's Will Is That Many Be Accounted Righteous and Intercession Be Made

It was God's will that His servant be crushed when He made an offering for guilt and sin, to make many accounted righteous as He bore all their iniquities and makes intercession for the transgressors (Isaiah 53:10-12).

The Promised Glory That God Be Glorified

Arise and shine! Although darkness covers the world, the Lord's glory will be seen upon you that the Lord be glorified and praised.

You will experience blessing and abundance, a work done by the Lord, and a planting done by the Lord, for His glory.

The Lord will be your everlasting light and God will be your glory (read Isaiah 60).

Isaiah 60:22 (GW)
> The smallest of them will become a family. The weakest of them will become a mighty nation. At the right time I, the LORD, will make it happen quickly."

Zion's Coming Salvation – The Lord's Delight, a Crown of Beauty in the Hand of the Lord

Isaiah 62:1-4
> For Zion's sake I will not keep silent, and for Jerusalem's sake I will not be quiet, until her righteousness goes forth as brightness, and her salvation as a burning torch. The nations shall see your righteousness, and all the kings your glory, and you shall be called by a new name that the mouth of the LORD will give.
>
> You shall be a crown of beauty in the hand of the LORD, and a royal diadem in the hand of your God. You shall no more be termed Forsaken, and your land shall no more be termed Desolate, but <u>you shall be called My Delight Is in Her</u>, and your land <u>Married</u>; for the LORD delights in you, and your land shall be married (also Isaiah 62:5-7).

Who Does God Look At?

The Lord says that heaven is His throne and the earth His footstool, but He looks to the one whose spirit is humble, receives correction, is teachable, and who trembles at His Word (Isaiah 66:1-2).

Micah (738-698 BC)

The Lord spoke through Micah during the days of Kings Jotham, Ahaz, and Hezekiah of Juda which he saw concerning Samaria and Jerusalem.

Again, the Lord cries out to those who plan to harm others (Micah 2:1).

Addressing the Lack of Good Leadership From the Rulers of Israel

The Lord addressed the leaders of Israel who hated the good and loved evil. They perverted everything that was right. They tore the skin off the Lord's people and the flesh from their bones. When these leaders cried to the Lord, He did not answer them, but hid His face from them because of their evil deeds (Micah 3:1-4).

Addressing the Lack of Good Leadership From the Prophets of Israel

The Lord also spoke through the prophet Micah about the prophets who were leading His people astray.

Micah 3:5-7 (GW)
>This is what the LORD says about the prophets who mislead my people: When they have something to eat, they say, "All is well!" But they declare a holy war against those who don't feed them.
>
>That is why you will have nights without visions. You will have darkness without revelations. The sun will set on the prophets, and the day will turn dark for them. Seers will be put to shame. Those who practice witchcraft will be disgraced. All of them will cover their faces, because God won't answer them.

The Mountain of the Lord

The Lord declared that in the latter days, the mountain of the house of the Lord shall be established as the highest mountain, and all peoples shall flow to it. Many nations shall come for the Lord to teach them His ways and show them how to walk in them (Micah 4:1-5).

The Lame and Afflicted

Micah 4:6-7
>"In that day, declares the LORD, I will assemble the lame and gather those who have been driven away and those whom I have afflicted; and the lame I will make the remnant, and those who were cast off, a strong

nation; <u>and the LORD will reign over them in Mount Zion from this time forth and forevermore</u>."

The Messiah Shall Be Born in Bethlehem and Be Shepherd of His Flock

From Bethlehem shall come the ruler in Israel, whose coming forth is from old, from ancient days. He shall stand and shepherd His flock in the strength of the Lord, and the majesty of the name of the Lord, His God. He shall be great to the ends of the earth and He shall be their peace (Micah 5:2-5).

What Does the Lord Require of You?

Micah 6:8
> He has told you, O man, what is good; and what does the LORD require of you but to <u>do justice</u>, and to <u>love kindness</u>, and to <u>walk humbly with your God</u>?

God's Steadfast Love and Compassion

Micah 7:18-20 (GW)
> Who is a God like You? You forgive sin and overlook the rebellion of your faithful people. You will not be angry forever, because You would rather show mercy. You will again have compassion on us. You will overcome our wrongdoing. You will throw all our sins into the deep sea.
>
> You will be faithful to Jacob. You will have mercy on Abraham as you swore by an oath to our ancestors long ago.

Glory to Glory Q&A

The power of God is evident in how His word transforms lives. The Lord promised in Isaiah 55 that His word will not return to Him empty, but that it will fulfill a purpose.

1. Name one passage from the book of Isaiah that touched you deeply.
2. Name five things from Isaiah that gave you comfort and joy in the Lord.
3. What hope is there for you in Isaiah 54:17?
4. Name the three things that the Lord requires of you, according to the prophet Micah in Micah 6:8.
5. What are the three characteristics in a person that catch the Lord's attention according to prophet Isaiah in Isaiah 66:2?

Prophets Jeremiah, Ezekiel and Zephaniah

Jeremiah (650-582 BC)

Jeremiah 4:19-20&22 (ISV)
"My anguish, My anguish! I writhe in pain. Oh, the aching of My heart!

My heart pounds within Me; I cannot keep silent. For I hear the sound of the trumpet, the alarm for war. Disaster upon disaster is proclaimed, for the entire land is devastated. Suddenly My tent is destroyed, in a moment My curtains.

For My people are foolish, they don't know Me. They're stupid children, they have no understanding. They're skilled at doing evil, but how to do good, they don't know."

"Be horrified, O heavens, at this; be shocked, be utterly heart-broken", declares the LORD, "for My people have done two evils: they have rejected Me, the fountain of living waters, and they have carved out water-troughs for themselves, broken cisterns that cannot hold water" (Jeremiah 2:12-13).

Jeremiah's Instruction From the Lord

King Hezekiah of Judah was the last king that Isaiah prophesied to. He was succeeded by his son, King Manasseh (697-643) who performed extreme abominations in the sanctuary of the Lord, where the Lord had promised His eyes and ears will always be amidst His people. Jeremiah was born in 650 BC and he could have witnessed some of these atrocities as a young boy.

God appointed Jeremiah as His prophet and set him over nations and kingdoms, to pluck up and to break down, to destroy and overthrow, to build and to plant (Jeremiah 1:10).

He prophesied to Kings Josiah, his son Jehoiakim, and his son Zedekiah of Judah, until the captivity of Jerusalem and their exile to Babylon.

He personally witnessed the ruin of Jerusalem. In the book of Lamentations, he expresses his deep sorrow about Jerusalem, and places his hope in the Lord's steadfast love and mercy.

Because both Judah and Israel had been utterly unfaithful to the Lord, and their prophets just a whiff of air, who didn't have the word of God in them, the Lord made the words of Jeremiah like fire and the people like wood (Jeremiah 5:1-18).

The Lord declared that He would bring an ancient nation from the north, whose language they didn't understand, to consume and destroy Jerusalem and its people's harvests, flocks, herds, and children, because of what they brought upon themselves.

What did Judah and Israel do to bring such destruction upon themselves?

False Prophets

The Lord sent His prophets to warn the kings and priests, the leaders of His people, to correct them from doing wrong and leading His people astray.

The false prophets were trying to win the favor of the people by not conveying to them what the Lord said, but instead they tried to soothe them with nice words, saying "peace" when there was no peace.

They were speaking to them from their own minds and hearts, saying "declares the Lord", when the Lord didn't send them (see also Jeremiah 14:13-15 & Ezekiel 13).

Jeremiah 5:30-31 (ISV)
"An appalling and horrible thing has happened in the land: The prophets prophesy falsely, the priests rule by their own authority, and My people love it this way. But what will you do in the end?"

Jeremiah 23:16-31
Thus says the LORD of hosts: "Do not listen to the words of the prophets who prophesy to you, filling you with vain hopes. They speak visions of their own minds, not from the mouth of the LORD. They say continually

to those who despise the word of the LORD, 'It shall be well with you'; and to everyone who stubbornly follows his own heart, they say, 'No disaster shall come upon you.'"

For who among them has stood in the council of the LORD to see and to hear His word, or who has paid attention to His word and listened?

Behold, the storm of the LORD! Wrath has gone forth, a whirling tempest; it will burst upon the head of the wicked. The anger of the LORD will not turn back until He has executed and accomplished the intents of His heart. In the latter days you will understand it clearly.

I did not send the prophets, yet they ran; I did not speak to them, yet they prophesied. But if they had stood in My council, then they would have proclaimed My words to My people, and they would have turned them from their evil way, and from the evil of their deeds.

Am I a God at hand, declares the LORD, and not a God far away? Can a man hide himself in secret places so that I cannot see him? Do I not fill heaven and earth? declares the LORD.

I have heard what the prophets have said who <u>prophesy lies in My name</u>, saying, 'I have dreamed, I have dreamed!' How long shall there be lies in the heart of the prophets who prophesy lies, and who prophesy the deceit of their own heart, who think to make My people forget My name by their dreams that they tell one another, even as their fathers forgot My name for Baal?

Let the prophet who has a dream tell the dream, but let him who has My word speak My word faithfully. What has straw in common with wheat?" declares the LORD.

"Is not My word like fire", declares the LORD, and like a hammer that breaks the rock in pieces? Therefore, behold, I am against the prophets who steal My words from one another. Behold, I am against the prophets," declares the LORD," who use their tongues and declare, 'declares the LORD.'"

As mentioned in an earlier chapter, the prophets who were appointed by God each had an encounter with God, and received His counsel before they went out to speak. These prophets decreed and prophesied the words that they received from the Lord.

The Harm Done by a False Prophecy

False prophecy leads people astray and does not help them at all (Jeremiah 23:32)!

Ezekiel lived in Babylon, more or less during the same time that Jeremiah prophesied in Jerusalem. He declared the following from the Lord that would explain why people were being led astray.

Ezekiel 13:22
> Because you have disheartened the righteous falsely, although I have not grieved him, and you have encouraged the wicked, that he should not turn from his evil way to save his life,

This scripture right here is the core of God's indignation: He was being misrepresented where the people whom He loved deeply were discouraged and wounded by the false prophets as their hope in God was destroyed by their false words. People were discouraged by their oppression of the wicked ways of others, thinking that it was God's will when it wasn't Him who spoke.

Furthermore, the oppressors were not corrected, but rather encouraged to continue in their ways.

When God corrects, it is **always** out of love, to bring about goodness and life! (Hebrews 12:6-11)

The Condition of the Lord's People

The prophet Jeremiah declared from the Lord the condition of His people what He wanted to uproot and destroy. He also pleaded, on behalf of the Lord, to the people to turn away from wrongdoing, and he presented the Lord's outcome and hope.

Your One Night Continues

Bride of Christ, as your "one night with the King" continues, listen closely as He continues to share His heart with you:

They Left the Lord

Jeremiah 2:5-8
> Thus says the Lord: "What wrong did your fathers find in Me that they went far from Me, and went after worthlessness, and became worthless?
>
> They did not say, 'Where is the LORD who brought us up from the land of Egypt, who led us in the wilderness, in a land of deserts and pits, in a land of drought and deep darkness, in a land that none passes through, where no man dwells?' And I brought you into a plentiful land to enjoy its fruits and its good things. But when you came in, you defiled My land and made My heritage an abomination.

The priests did not say, 'Where is the LORD?' Those who handle the law did not know Me; the shepherds transgressed against Me; the prophets prophesied by Baal and went after things that do not profit."

They Changed Their Glory

"My people changed their glory, for that which does not profit" (Jeremiah 2:11).

They Played the Whore

"My beloved played the whore with many lovers, polluting the land. They turned away from Me to worship stone idols and foreign gods under trees. When they returned to Me, it was only in pretence and not from the heart" (Jeremiah 3:1-10).

They Did Not Defend the Needy

Jeremiah 5:27-29
> "Like a cage full of birds, their houses are full of deceit; therefore they have become great and rich; they have grown fat and sleek. They know no bounds in deeds of evil; they judge not with justice the cause of the fatherless, to make it prosper, and they do not defend the rights of the needy.
>
> Shall I not punish them for these things?" declares the LORD, "and shall I not avenge Myself on a nation such as this?"

They Were Greedy for Unjust Gain

Jeremiah 6:13-15
> "For from the least to the greatest of them, everyone is greedy for unjust gain; and from <u>prophet to priest, everyone deals falsely</u>. They have healed the wound of My people lightly, saying, 'Peace, peace,' when there is no peace.
>
> Were they ashamed when they committed abomination? No, they were not at all ashamed; they did not know how to blush. Therefore they shall fall among those who fall; at the time that I punish them, they shall be overthrown," says the LORD. (See also Jeremiah 9)

They Pursued Their Own, Stubborn Plans, Refusing Correction

Jeremiah 7:24-26&28
> "But they did not obey or incline their ear, but walked in their own counsels and the stubbornness of their evil hearts, and went backward and not forward. From the day that your fathers came out of the land of

Egypt to this day, I have persistently sent all My servants the prophets to them, day after day. Yet they did not listen to Me or incline their ear, but stiffened their neck. They did worse than their fathers.

And you shall say to them, 'This is the nation that did not obey the voice of the LORD their God, and did not accept discipline; truth has perished; it is cut off from their lips.'"

They Lied

Jeremiah 9:3
"They bend their tongue like a bow; falsehood and not truth has grown strong in the land; for they proceed from evil to evil, and they do not know Me," declares the LORD.

Jeremiah 9:5-8
"Everyone deceives his neighbour, and no one speaks the truth; they have taught their tongue to speak lies; they weary themselves committing iniquity. Heaping oppression upon oppression, and deceit upon deceit, they refuse to know Me," declares the LORD.

Therefore thus says the LORD of hosts: "Behold, I will refine them and test them, for what else can I do, because of My people? Their tongue is a deadly arrow; it speaks deceitfully; with his mouth each speaks peace to his neighbour, but in his heart he plans an ambush for him."

Stupid Shepherds Didn't Ask God's Guidance

Jeremiah 10:21
For the shepherds are stupid and do not inquire of the LORD; therefore they have not prospered, and all their flock is scattered. (See also Jeremiah 23:1-2)

They Broke Covenant With the Lord

Jeremiah 11:9-17
Again the LORD said to me (Jeremiah), "A conspiracy exists among the men of Judah and the inhabitants of Jerusalem. They have turned back to the iniquities of their forefathers, who refused to hear My words. They have gone after other gods to serve them. The house of Israel and the house of Judah have broken My covenant that I made with their fathers. Therefore, thus says the LORD, Behold, I am bringing disaster upon them that they cannot escape. Though they cry to Me, I will not listen to them. Then the cities of Judah and the inhabitants of Jerusalem will go and cry to the gods to whom they make offerings, but they cannot save them in the time of their trouble.

For your gods have become as many as your cities, O Judah, and as many as the streets of Jerusalem are the altars you have set up to shame, altars to make offerings to Baal.

Therefore do not pray for this people, or lift up a cry or prayer on their behalf, for I will not listen when they call to Me in the time of their trouble. What right has My beloved in My house, when she has done many vile deeds? Can even sacrificial flesh avert your doom? Can you then exult?

The LORD once called you 'a green olive tree, beautiful with good fruit.' But with the roar of a great tempest He will set fire to it, and its branches will be consumed.

The LORD of hosts, who planted you, has decreed disaster against you, because of the evil that the house of Israel and the house of Judah have done, provoking Me to anger by making offerings to Baal."

The Evil of Pride

Jeremiah 13:8-11

Then the word of the LORD came to me: "Thus says the LORD: "Even so will I spoil the pride of Judah and the great pride of Jerusalem.

This evil people, who refuse to hear My words, who stubbornly follow their own heart and have gone after other gods to serve them and worship them, shall be like this loincloth, which is good for nothing.

For as the loincloth clings to the waist of a man, so I made the whole house of Israel and the whole house of Judah cling to Me, declares the LORD, that they might be for Me a people, a name, a praise, and a glory, but they would not listen."

They Have Forsaken the Fountain of Living Water

Jeremiah 17:12-13

A glorious throne set on high from the beginning is the place of our sanctuary. O LORD, the hope of Israel, all who forsake You shall be put to shame; those who turn away from You shall be written in the earth, for they have forsaken the LORD, the fountain of living water.

Trusting in the Flesh of Man, or in the Lord?

Jeremiah 17:5-8

Thus says the LORD: "Cursed is the man who trusts in man and makes flesh his strength, whose heart turns away from the LORD. He is like a shrub in the desert, and shall not see any good come. He shall dwell in the parched places of the wilderness, in an uninhabited salt land.

Blessed is the man who trusts in the LORD, whose trust is the LORD. He is like a tree planted by water, that sends out its roots by the stream, and does not fear when heat comes, for its leaves remain green, and is not anxious in the year of drought, for it does not cease to bear fruit."

God Explains His Wrath Against Abominations Done, That Did Not Even Enter His Mind!

Jeremiah 32:26-35 (ISV)
Then this message from the LORD came to Jeremiah:

"Look, I am the LORD, the God who rules over all flesh. Is anything too difficult for me?"

Therefore, this is what the LORD says: "I'm about to give this city into the hands of the Chaldeans and Nebuchadnezzar, king of Babylon, and he will capture it. The Chaldeans who are fighting against this city will come, set this city on fire, and burn it along with the houses on whose roofs incense was burned to Baal and liquid offerings were poured out to other gods in order to provoke me.

Indeed, the Israelis and Judeans have been doing only evil in My presence since their youth. Indeed, the Israelis have done nothing but provoke Me by what they have made with their hands," declares the LORD.

"Indeed, this city has provoked Me to anger and wrath from the day they built it until now, and so I'll remove it from My sight because of all the evil that the Israelis and Judeans have done to provoke Me. They, their kings, their officials, their priests, their prophets, the people of Judah, and those living in Jerusalem have done these things.

They have turned their backs to Me rather than their faces. Even though I taught them, teaching them again and again, they didn't listen to accept correction.

They put their detestable idols in the house that is called by My name and defiled it.

They built the high places of Baal that are in the Hinnom Valley in order to sacrifice their sons and daughters to Molech - <u>something that I didn't command, nor did it ever enter My mind</u> for them to require this utterly repugnant thing – and lead Judah into sin."

How the Lord Pleaded With His People

Return!

"Return, faithless Israel! I will not be angry forever, for I am merciful. Circumcise your hearts and acknowledge your guilt, that you rebelled against the Lord your God and scattered your favors among foreigners under every green tree, and that you have not obeyed My voice," pleaded the LORD (Jeremiah 3:11-15, and Jeremiah 4:4).

Search for Someone Who Is Truthful!

Jeremiah 5:1-5
> "Run to and fro through the streets of Jerusalem, look and take note! Search her squares to see if you can find a man, one who does justice and seeks truth, that I may pardon her. Though they say, 'As the LORD lives,' yet they swear falsely."
>
> O LORD, do not Your eyes look for truth? You have struck them down, but they felt no anguish; you have consumed them, but they refused to take correction. They have made their faces harder than rock; they have refused to repent.
>
> Then I said, "These are only the poor; they have no sense; for they do not know the way of the LORD, the justice of their God. I will go to the great and will speak to them, for they know the way of the LORD, the justice of their God."
>
> But they all alike had broken the yoke; they had burst the bonds.

"I Have Seen What You Are Doing"

Jeremiah 7:1-7 (GW)
> The LORD spoke His word to Jeremiah. He said, "Stand at the gate of the LORD'S house, and announce from there this message: 'Listen to the word of the LORD, all you people of Judah who go through these gates to worship the LORD.
>
> This is what the LORD of Armies, the God of Israel, says: Change the way you live and act, and I will let you live in this place.
>
> Do not trust the words of this saying, "This is the LORD'S temple, the LORD'S temple, the LORD'S temple!" It's a lie.
>
> Suppose you really change the way you live and act and you really treat each other fairly.

Suppose you do not oppress foreigners, orphans, and widows, or kill anyone in this place. And suppose you do not follow other gods that lead you to your own destruction.

Then I will let you live in this place, in the land that I gave permanently to your ancestors long ago.'"

Jeremiah 7:9-11 (GW)
"You steal, murder, commit adultery, lie when you take oaths, burn incense as an offering to Baal, and run after other gods that you do not know.

Then you stand in My presence in the house that is called by My name. You think that you're safe to do all these disgusting things.

The house that is called by My name has become a gathering place for thieves. I have seen what you are doing," declares the LORD.

Obey and Prosper

Jeremiah 7:22-23
"For in the day that I brought them out of the land of Egypt, I did not speak to your fathers or command them concerning burnt offerings and sacrifices. But this command I gave them: 'Obey My voice, and I will be your God, and you shall be My people. And walk in all the way that I command you, that it may be well with you.'"

The Outcome of Judah's Faithlessness and the Future Hope

An End

Jeremiah 4:27-28
For thus says the LORD, "The whole land shall be a desolation; yet I will not make a full end. "For this the earth shall mourn, and the heavens above be dark; for I have spoken; I have purposed; I have not relented, nor will I turn back." (See also Jeremiah 5:18)

Jeremiah 4:18
"Your ways and your deeds have brought this upon you. This is your doom, and it is bitter; it has reached your very heart."

Jeremiah 16:21
"Therefore, behold, I will make them know, this once I will make them know My power and My might, and they shall know that My name is the LORD."

When Boasting, Boast in Knowing the Lord

Jeremiah 9:23-24
> Thus says the LORD: "Let not the wise man boast in his wisdom, let not the mighty man boast in his might, let not the rich man boast in his riches, but let him who boasts boast in this, that he understands and knows Me, that I am the LORD who practices steadfast love, justice, and righteousness in the earth. For in these things I delight," declares the LORD.

There is None Like God

Jeremiah 10:5
> "Their idols are like scarecrows in a cucumber field, and they cannot speak; they have to be carried, for they cannot walk. Do not be afraid of them, for they cannot do evil, neither is it in them to do good."

Jeremiah 10:10
> But the LORD is the true God; He is the living God and the everlasting King. At His wrath the earth quakes, and the nations cannot endure His indignation.

Jeremiah 10:12-13
> It is He who made the earth by His power, who established the world by His wisdom, and by His understanding stretched out the heavens. When He utters His voice, there is a tumult of waters in the heavens, and He makes the mist rise from the ends of the earth. He makes lightning for the rain, and He brings forth the wind from His storehouses.

The Lamb (Jesus) to Be Led to the Slaughter

Jeremiah 11:18-19
> The LORD made it known to Me and I knew; then you showed Me their deeds. But I was like a gentle lamb led to the slaughter. I did not know it was against Me they devised schemes, saying, "Let us destroy the tree with its fruit, let us cut Him off from the land of the living, that His name be remembered no more."

Fishers of Men

"Behold, I am sending for many fishers," declares the LORD, "and they shall catch them" (Jeremiah 16:16).

The Lord Searches the Heart and Tests the Mind

Jeremiah 17:9-10

The heart is deceitful above all things, and desperately sick; who can understand it? "I the LORD search the heart and test the mind, to give every man according to his ways, according to the fruit of his deeds."

Gathering the Remnant of the Flock

Jeremiah 23:3-4

Then I will gather the remnant of My flock out of all the countries where I have driven them, and I will bring them back to their fold, and they shall be fruitful and multiply .I will set shepherds over them who will care for them, and they shall fear no more, nor be dismayed, neither shall any be missing, declares the LORD. (See also Jeremiah 3:15)

Jeremiah 29:10-13 (ISV)

"For this is what the LORD says: 'When Babylon's seventy years are completed, I'll take note of you and will fulfill My good promises to you by bringing you back to this place.

For I know the plans that I have for you', declares the LORD, 'plans for well-being, and not for calamity, in order to give you a future and a hope.

When you call out to Me and come and pray to Me, I'll hear you.

You will seek Me and find Me when you search for Me with all your heart.

The Righteous Branch From David Shall Reign as King!

Jeremiah 23:5-6

"Behold, the days are coming, declares the LORD, when I will raise up for David a righteous Branch, and He shall reign as king and deal wisely, and shall execute justice and righteousness in the land. In His days Judah will be saved, and Israel will dwell securely. And this is the name by which He will be called: **'The LORD is our righteousness.'"** (also Jeremiah 33:14-18, 24-26&Jeremiah 31)

The New Covenant, Not Like the One Israel and Judah Broke

Jeremiah 31:31-32

"Behold, the days are coming," declares the LORD, "when I will make a **new covenant** with the house of Israel and the house of Judah, not like the covenant that I made with their fathers on the day when I took them by the hand to bring them out of the land of Egypt, My covenant that they broke, though I was their husband," declares the LORD.

God's Ways Written on Hearts and Minds

Jeremiah 31:33-34

"For this is the covenant that I will make with the house of Israel after those days, declares the LORD: I will put My law within them, and I will write it on their hearts. And I will be their God, and they shall be My people. And no longer shall each one teach his neighbor and each his brother, saying, 'Know the LORD,' for they shall all know Me, from the least of them to the greatest, declares the LORD. For I will forgive their iniquity, and I will remember their sin no more."

God Will Give Them One Heart and One Way

Jeremiah 32:37-39 (ISV)

"I'm about to gather My people from all the lands where I've driven them in My anger, wrath, and great indignation. I'll bring them back to this place and let them live in safety.

They'll be My people, and I'll be their God.

I'll give them one heart and one lifestyle so they'll fear Me always for their own good and for the good of their descendants after them."

The Lord's Everlasting Covenant to Do Good to Them

Jeremiah 32:40-42

"I will make with them an everlasting covenant, that I will not turn away from doing good to them. And I will put the fear of Me in their hearts, that they may not turn from Me. I will rejoice in doing them good, and I will plant them in this land in faithfulness, with all My heart and all My soul.

For thus says the LORD: Just as I have brought all this great disaster upon this people, so I will bring upon them all the good that I promise them."

The Lord Promises Peace and Security, and to Cleanse Them From Their Guilt of Sin

Jeremiah 33:3-9

"Call to Me and I will answer you, and will tell you great and hidden things that you have not known."

For thus says the LORD, the God of Israel, concerning the houses of this city and the houses of the kings of Judah that were torn down to make a defence against the siege mounds and against the sword:

"They are coming in to fight against the Chaldeans and to fill them with the dead bodies of men whom I shall strike down in My anger and My wrath, for I have hidden My face from this city because of all their evil.

Behold, I will bring to it health and healing, and I will heal them and reveal to them abundance of prosperity and security. I will restore the fortunes of Judah and the fortunes of Israel, and rebuild them as they were at first.

I will cleanse them from all the guilt of their sin against Me, and I will forgive all the guilt of their sin and rebellion against Me. And this city shall be to Me a name of joy, a praise and a glory before all the nations of the earth who shall hear of all the good that I do for them. They shall fear and tremble because of all the good and all the prosperity I provide for it."

Ezekiel (620 – 570 BC)

The magnificent glory of the Lord appeared to Ezekiel and the Lord called him and sent him to the people of Israel who rebelled against Him (Ezekiel 1 is a must read).

The Lord warned him that they might refuse to listen, because they were rebellious. He told Ezekiel not to be afraid even when trampling on scorpions, but to speak His words whether they hear, or refuse to hear, for they were a rebellious house (Ezekiel 2).

The Lord showed him Jerusalem where He set her in the centre of the nations, with countries all around her. He told Ezekiel that in her rebellion, she did more wickedness than the countries around her, for they rejected the Lord's rules and did not walk in His ways, or according to His values. That was why even the Lord was against her, and He was going to execute judgments in her midst in the sight of all the nations (Ezekiel 5).

Because They Defiled His Intimate Sanctuary

For the likes of what Manasseh had done in the Lord's sanctuary.

Ezekiel 5:11-17

"Therefore, as I live, declares the Lord GOD, surely, because you have defiled My sanctuary with all your detestable things and with all your abominations, therefore I will withdraw. My eye will not spare, and I will have no pity. A third part of you shall die of pestilence and be consumed with famine in your midst; a third part shall fall by the sword all around you; and a third part I will scatter to all the winds and will unsheathe the sword after them.

Thus shall My anger spend itself, and I will vent My fury upon them and satisfy Myself. And they shall know that I am the LORD – that I have spoken in My jealousy – when I spend my fury upon them. Moreover, I will make you a desolation and an object of reproach among the nations all around you and in the sight of all who pass by.

You shall be a reproach and a taunt, a warning and a horror, to the nations all around you, when I execute judgments on you in anger and fury, and with furious rebukes – I am the LORD; I have spoken – when I send against you the deadly arrows of famine, arrows for destruction, which I will send to destroy you, and when I bring more and more famine upon you and break your supply of bread. I will send famine and wild beasts against you, and they will rob you of your children. Pestilence and blood shall pass through you, and I will bring the sword upon you. I am the LORD; I have spoken."

An End Has Come

Ezekiel 7:1-3
> The word of the LORD came to me: "And you, O son of man, thus says the Lord GOD to the land of Israel: An end! The end has come upon the four corners of the land. Now the end is upon you, and I will send My anger upon you; I will judge you according to your ways, and I will punish you for all your abominations."

End to the Pride

Ezekiel 7:24-25
> I will bring the worst of the nations to take possession of their houses. I will put an end to the pride of the strong, and their holy places shall be profaned. When anguish comes, they will seek peace, but there shall be none.

A definition of pride is: a feeling of "deep pleasure and satisfaction obtained from one's own achievements."

Pride is to reject the gifts that God has freely given by focusing on one's own efforts and building one's own kingdom rather than His kingdom.

The Things Done Secretly in the Temple, the Home of the Lord

Ezekiel was in his house, with the elders of Israel with him, when the hand of the Lord fell upon him there:

Ezekiel 8:2-18

> Then I looked, and behold, a form that had the appearance of a man. Below what appeared to be his waist was fire, and above his waist was something like the appearance of brightness, like gleaming metal. He put out the form of a hand and took me by a lock of my head, and the Spirit lifted me up between earth and heaven and brought me in visions of God to Jerusalem, to the entrance of the gateway of the inner court that faces north, where was the seat of the image of jealousy, which provokes to jealousy.
>
> And behold, the glory of the God of Israel was there, like the vision that I saw in the valley. Then He said to me, "Son of man, lift up your eyes now toward the north." So I lifted up my eyes toward the north, and behold, north of the altar gate, in the entrance, was this image of jealousy.
>
> And He said to me, "Son of man, do you see what they are doing, the great abominations that the house of Israel are committing here, to drive Me far from My sanctuary? But you will see still greater abominations."
>
> And he brought me to the entrance of the court, and when I looked, behold, there was a hole in the wall. Then He said to me, "Son of man, dig in the wall." So I dug in the wall, and behold, there was an entrance. And He said to me, "Go in, and see the vile abominations that they are committing here."
>
> So I went in and saw. And there, engraved on the wall all around, was every form of creeping things and loathsome beasts, and all the idols of the house of Israel. And before them stood seventy men of the elders of the house of Israel, with Jaazaniah the son of Shaphan standing among them. Each had his censer in his hand, and the smoke of the cloud of incense went up.
>
> Then He said to me, "Son of man, have you seen what the elders of the house of Israel are doing in the dark, each in his room of pictures? For they say, 'The LORD does not see us, the LORD has forsaken the land.'"
>
> He said also to me, "You will see still greater abominations that they commit."
>
> Then he brought me to the entrance of the north gate of the house of the LORD, and behold, there sat women weeping for Tammuz. Then He said to me, "Have you seen this, O son of man? You will see still greater abominations than these."
>
> And He brought me into the inner court of the house of the LORD. And behold, at the entrance of the temple of the LORD, between the porch and the altar, were about twenty-five men, with their backs to the temple

of the LORD, and their faces toward the east, worshiping the sun toward the east.

Then He said to me, "Have you seen this, O son of man? Is it too light a thing for the house of Judah to commit the abominations that they commit here, that they should fill the land with violence and provoke Me still further to anger? Behold, they put the branch to their nose. Therefore I will act in wrath. My eye will not spare, nor will I have pity. And though they cry in My ears with a loud voice, I will not hear them."

Mark for Protection Those Who Are Filled With Sorrow Over the Abominations, and Wipe Out the Idolaters

Ezekiel 9:1-11

Then he cried in my ears with a loud voice, saying, "Bring near the executioners of the city, each with his destroying weapon in his hand." And behold, six men came from the direction of the upper gate, which faces north, each with his weapon for slaughter in his hand, and with them was a man clothed in linen, with a writing case at his waist. And they went in and stood beside the bronze altar.

Now the glory of the God of Israel had gone up from the cherub on which it rested to the threshold of the house. And he called to the man clothed in linen, who had the writing case at his waist. And the LORD said to him, "Pass through the city, through Jerusalem, and put a mark on the foreheads of the men who sigh and groan over all the abominations that are committed in it."

And to the others he said in my hearing, "Pass through the city after him, and strike. Your eye shall not spare, and you shall show no pity. Kill old men outright, young men and maidens, little children and women, but touch no one on whom is the mark. And begin at My sanctuary." So they began with the elders who were before the house.

Then he said to them, "Defile the house, and fill the courts with the slain. Go out." So they went out and struck in the city. And while they were striking, and I was left alone, I fell upon my face, and cried, "Ah, Lord GOD! Will You destroy all the remnant of Israel in the outpouring of Your wrath on Jerusalem?"

Then He said to me, "The guilt of the house of Israel and Judah is exceedingly great. The land is full of blood, and the city full of injustice. For they say, 'The LORD has forsaken the land, and the LORD does not see.' As for Me, My eye will not spare, nor will I have pity; I will bring their deeds upon their heads."

And behold, the man clothed in linen, with the writing case at his waist, brought back word, saying, "I have done as You commanded me."

God's Glory Left the Temple

Ezekiel 10:18-22
> Then the glory of the LORD went out from the threshold of the house, and stood over the cherubim. And the cherubim lifted up their wings and mounted up from the earth before my eyes as they went out, with the wheels beside them. And they stood at the entrance of the east gate of the house of the LORD, and the glory of the God of Israel was over them.
>
> These were the living creatures that I saw underneath the God of Israel by the Chebar canal (see also Ezekiel 1); and I knew that they were cherubim. Each had four faces, and each four wings, and underneath their wings the likeness of human hands. And as for the likeness of their faces, they were the same faces whose appearance I had seen by the Chebar canal. Each one of them went straight forward.

Though I Have Scattered Them, I Have Been a Sanctuary to Them

Ezekiel 11:16
> Therefore say, 'Thus says the Lord GOD: Though I removed them far off among the nations, and though I scattered them among the countries, yet I have been a sanctuary to them for a while in the countries where they have gone.'

Empowered to Obey

Giving Them a New Heart and a New Spirit

Ezekiel 11:17-21
> Therefore say, 'Thus says the Lord GOD: I will gather you from the peoples and assemble you out of the countries where you have been scattered, and I will give you the land of Israel.' And when they come there, they will remove from it all its detestable things and all its abominations. And I will give them one heart, and a new spirit I will put within them.
>
> I will remove the heart of stone from their flesh and give them a heart of flesh, that they may walk in My statutes and keep My rules and obey them. And they shall be My people, and I will be their God.
>
> But as for those whose heart goes after their detestable things and their abominations, I will bring their deeds upon their own heads,' declares the Lord GOD.

Their hearts of stone were worshipping stony idols having their hearts hardened against the Lord, but hearts of flesh will be vulnerable and humble to worship and adore their Maker.

The Lord's Everlasting Covenant of Atonement, Despite of Them Breaking Covenant

Ezekiel 16:59-60
> For thus says the Lord GOD: "I will deal with you as you have done, you who have despised the oath in breaking the covenant, yet I will remember My covenant with you in the days of your youth, and I will establish for you an everlasting covenant."

Ezekiel 16:62-63
> "<u>I will establish My covenant with you, and you shall know that I am the LORD</u>, that you may remember and be confounded, and never open your mouth again because of your shame, <u>when I atone for you for all that you have done</u>," declares the Lord GOD.

Who is able to love like the Lord? His mercy and steadfast love endures forever. Jesus, who knew no sin, became sin that in Him we may become the righteousness of God (2 Corinthians 5:18-21).

Turn (Repent) and Live, for the Lord Has No Pleasure in the Death of Anyone

Ezekiel 18:27-32
> "Again, when a wicked person turns away from the wickedness he has committed and does what is just and right, he shall save his life. Because he considered and turned away from all the transgressions that he had committed, he shall surely live; he shall not die.
>
> Yet the house of Israel says, 'The way of the Lord is not just.' O house of Israel, are My ways not just? Is it not your ways that are not just? Therefore I will judge you, O house of Israel, every one according to his ways," declares the Lord GOD.
>
> "Repent and turn from all your transgressions, lest iniquity be your ruin. Cast away from you all the transgressions that you have committed, and make yourselves a new heart and a new spirit! Why will you die, O house of Israel? <u>For I have no pleasure in the death of anyone, declares the Lord GOD; so turn, and live.</u>" (See also Ezekiel 33:10-11)

My Holy Name You Shall No More Profane (Drag Through the Mud)

Ezekiel 20:36-39

"As I entered into judgment with your fathers in the wilderness of the land of Egypt, so I will enter into judgment with you," declares the Lord GOD. "I will make you pass under the rod, and I will bring you into the bond of the covenant.

I will purge out the rebels from among you, and those who transgress against Me. I will bring them out of the land where they sojourn, but they shall not enter the land of Israel. Then you will know that I am the LORD."

As for you, O house of Israel, thus says the Lord GOD: "Go serve every one of you his idols, now and hereafter, if you will not listen to Me; but My holy name you shall no more profane (drag through the mud) with your gifts and your idols."

The Dross of Silver in the Fire

Ezekiel 22:17-22

And the word of the LORD came to me: "Son of man, the house of Israel has become dross to Me; all of them are bronze and tin and iron and lead in the furnace; they are dross of silver.

Therefore thus says the Lord GOD: Because you have all become dross, therefore, behold, I will gather you into the midst of Jerusalem. As one gathers silver and bronze and iron and lead and tin into a furnace, to blow the fire on it in order to melt it, so I will gather you in My anger and in My wrath, and I will put you in and melt you.

I will gather you and blow on you with the fire of My wrath, and you shall be melted in the midst of it. As silver is melted in a furnace, so you shall be melted in the midst of it, and you shall know that I am the LORD; I have poured out My wrath upon you."

This Is the Dross – The Reason for God's Indignation

Ezekiel 22:25-29

"The conspiracy of her prophets in her midst is like a roaring lion tearing the prey; they have devoured human lives; they have taken treasure and precious things; they have made many widows in her midst.

Her priests have done violence to My law and have profaned My holy things. They have made no distinction between the holy and the common, neither have they taught the difference between the unclean and the clean, and they have disregarded My Sabbaths, so that I am profaned among them.

Her <u>princes</u> in her midst are like wolves tearing the prey, shedding blood, destroying lives to get dishonest gain.

And her <u>prophets</u> have smeared whitewash for them, seeing false visions and divining lies for them, saying, 'Thus says the Lord GOD,' when the LORD has not spoken.

The <u>people</u> of the land have practiced extortion and committed robbery. They have oppressed the poor and needy, and have extorted from the sojourner without justice."

There Was No One to Intercede for Them

Ezekiel 22:30-31

"And I sought for a man among them who should build up the wall and stand in the breach before Me for the land, that I should not destroy it, but I found none.

Therefore I have poured out My indignation upon them. I have consumed them with the fire of My wrath. I have returned their way upon their heads," declares the Lord GOD.

The Lord God Himself Will Seek Out His Sheep

Ezekiel 34:11-24

For thus says the Lord GOD: "Behold, I, I Myself will search for My sheep and will seek them out. As a shepherd seeks out his flock when he is among his sheep that have been scattered, so will I seek out My sheep, and I will rescue them from all places where they have been scattered on a day of clouds and thick darkness.

And I will bring them out from the peoples and gather them from the countries, and will bring them into their own land. And I will feed them on the mountains of Israel, by the ravines, and in all the inhabited places of the country.

I will feed them with good pasture, and on the mountain heights of Israel shall be their grazing land. There they shall lie down in good grazing land, and on rich pasture they shall feed on the mountains of Israel.

I Myself will be the shepherd of My sheep, and I Myself will make them lie down, declares the Lord GOD. I will seek the lost, and I will bring back the strayed, and I will bind up the injured, and I will strengthen the weak, and the fat and the strong I will destroy. I will feed them in justice.

As for you, My flock," thus says the Lord GOD: "Behold, I judge between sheep and sheep, between rams and male goats.

Is it not enough for you to feed on the good pasture, that you must tread down with your feet the rest of your pasture; and to drink of clear water, that you must muddy the rest of the water with your feet?

And must My sheep eat what you have trodden with your feet, and drink what you have muddied with your feet?" Therefore, thus says the Lord GOD to them: "Behold, I, I Myself will judge between the fat sheep and the lean sheep.

Because you push with side and shoulder, and thrust at all the weak with your horns, till you have scattered them abroad, I will rescue My flock; they shall no longer be a prey. And I will judge between sheep and sheep.

And I will set up over them one shepherd, My servant David, and He shall feed them: He shall feed them and be their shepherd. And I, the LORD, will be their God, and My servant David shall be prince among them. I am the LORD; I have spoken."

The Lord's Covenant of Peace

Ezekiel 34:25-31 (GW)
"I will promise them peace. I will remove the wild animals from the land so that my sheep can live safely in the wilderness and sleep in the woods.

I will bless them and the places around My hill. I will send rain at the right time. These showers will be a blessing to them.

Then the trees in the field will produce fruit, the land will yield crops, and My sheep will live safely in their land. Then they will know that I am the LORD, because I will break off the bars on their yokes and rescue them from the people who made them slaves.

They will no longer be prey to the nations, and the wild animals will no longer eat them. They will live safely, and no one will frighten them.

I will give them a place that is known for its good crops. They will no longer experience hunger in the land, and they will no longer suffer the insults of other nations.

Then they will know that I, the LORD their God, am with them and that they, the people of Israel, are My people, declares the Almighty LORD.

You, My sheep, are the sheep in My pasture. You are mortal, and I am your God", declares the Almighty LORD.

Israel Degraded the Lord's Name Amongst the Nations

Ezekiel 36:16-21

> The word of the LORD came to me: "Son of man, when the house of Israel lived in their own land, they defiled it by their ways and their deeds. Their ways before Me were like the uncleanness of a woman in her menstrual impurity.
>
> So I poured out My wrath upon them for the blood that they had shed in the land, for the idols with which they had defiled it. I scattered them among the nations, and they were dispersed through the countries. In accordance with their ways and their deeds I judged them.
>
> But when they came to the nations, wherever they came, they profaned My holy name, in that people said of them, 'These are the people of the LORD, and yet they had to go out of His land.' But I had concern for My holy name, which the house of Israel had profaned among the nations to which they came."

I Will Put My Spirit Within You for the Sake of My Holy Name

Ezekiel 36:22-38 (ISV)

> Therefore tell the house of Israel, This is what the Lord GOD says: "I'm not about to act for your sake, you house of Israel, but for the sake of My holy reputation, which you have been defiling throughout all of the nations where you've gone.
>
> I'm going to affirm My great reputation that has been defiled among the nations (that is, that you have defiled in their midst), and those people will learn that I am the LORD," declares the Lord GOD, "when I affirm My holiness in front of their very eyes.
>
> I'm going to remove you from the nations, gather you from all of the territories, and bring you all back to your own land.
>
> I'll sprinkle pure water on you all, and you'll be cleansed from your impurity and from all of your idols.
>
> I'm going to give you a new heart, and I'm going to give you a new spirit within all of your deepest parts. I'll remove that rock-hard heart of yours and replace it with one that's sensitive to Me.
>
> I'll place My spirit within you, empowering you to live according to My regulations and to keep My just decrees.
>
> You'll live in the land that I gave to your ancestors, you'll be My people, and I will be your God.

In addition, I'll deliver you from everything that makes you unclean. I'll call out to the grain you plant, ordering it to produce abundant yields, and I will never bring famine in your direction.

I'll increase the yields of your fruit trees and crops so that you'll never again experience the disgrace of famine that occurs in other nations.

Then you'll remember your lifestyles and practices that were not good. You'll hate yourselves as you look at your own iniquities and loathsome practices.

I won't be doing any of this for your sake," declares the Lord GOD, "so keep that in mind. Be ashamed and frustrated because of your behavior, you house of Israel!"

This is what the Lord GOD says: "At the same time that I cleanse you from all of your guilt, I'll make your cities become inhabited again and the desolate wastelands will be rebuilt.

The desolate fields will be cultivated, replacing the former wasteland that everyone who passed by in times past had noticed.

They will say, 'This wasteland has become like the garden of Eden, and what used to be desolate ruins are now fortified and inhabited.'

Then the surviving people that live around you will learn that I, the LORD, have rebuilt these ruins and have cultivated these pastures that used to be desolate wastelands. I, the LORD, have spoken this, and I'm going to bring it about!"

This is what the Lord GOD has to say: "I'm going to allow the house of Israel to ask anything they want from Me, including this: I'm going to increase their population as a shepherd increases his flock.

The desolate cities will be filled with flocks of human beings, just like Jerusalem used to be filled with flocks of sheep during the times of the appointed feasts. Then they will know that I am the LORD."

One Nation

God will join Judah and Israel together, that they will be one in the hand of the Lord (Ezekiel 37).

They shall not defile themselves anymore with their idols, but I will save them from all the backslidings and transgressions, and will cleanse them; and they shall be My people, and I will be their God.

Ezekiel 37:24-28
> "<u>My servant David shall be king over them, and they shall all have one shepherd</u>. They shall walk in My rules and be careful to obey My statutes.
>
> They shall dwell in the land that I gave to My servant Jacob, where your fathers lived. They and their children and their children's children shall dwell there forever, and David My servant shall be their prince forever.
>
> I will make a covenant of peace with them. It shall be an everlasting covenant with them. And I will set them in their land and multiply them, and will set My sanctuary in their midst forevermore. (See also Ezekiel 40-48)
>
> My dwelling place shall be with them, and I will be their God, and they shall be My people.
>
> Then the nations will know that I am the LORD who sanctifies Israel, when My sanctuary is in their midst forevermore."

Ezekiel 39:29
> And <u>I will not hide My face anymore from them, when I pour out My Spirit upon the house of Israel</u>, declares the Lord GOD.

The Name of the City

Ezekiel 48:35
> The circumference of the city shall be 18,000 cubits. And the name of the city from that time on shall be, **The LORD Is There.**"

Zephaniah (640 – 626 BC)

The Conversion of the Nations

Zephaniah 3:9-13
> "For at that time I will change the speech of the peoples to a pure speech, that all of them may call upon the name of the LORD and serve Him with one accord.
>
> From beyond the rivers of Cush My worshipers, the daughter of My dispersed ones, shall bring My offering.
>
> On that day you shall not be put to shame because of the deeds by which you have rebelled against Me; for then I will remove from your midst your proudly exultant ones, and you shall no longer be haughty in My holy mountain.
>
> But I will leave in your midst a people humble and lowly. They shall seek refuge in the name of the LORD, those who are left in Israel; they

shall do no injustice and speak no lies, nor shall there be found in their mouth a deceitful tongue. For they shall graze and lie down, and none shall make them afraid."

Israel's Joy and Restoration

Zephaniah 3:14-20

Sing aloud, O daughter of Zion; shout, O Israel! Rejoice and exult with all your heart, O daughter of Jerusalem!

The LORD has taken away the judgments against you; He has cleared away your enemies. The King of Israel, the LORD, is in your midst; you shall never again fear evil. On that day it shall be said to Jerusalem: "Fear not, O Zion; let not your hands grow weak.

The LORD your God is in your midst, a mighty one who will save; He will rejoice over you with gladness; He will quiet you by His love; He will exult over you with loud singing.

I will gather those of you who mourn for the festival, so that you will no longer suffer reproach. Behold, at that time I will deal with all your oppressors. And I will save the lame and gather the outcast, and I will change their shame into praise and renown in all the earth.

At that time I will bring you in, at the time when I gather you together; for I will make you renowned and praised among all the peoples of the earth, when I restore your fortunes before your eyes," says the LORD.

"I will put My law within them, and I will write it on their hearts. And I will be their God, and they shall be My people. And no longer shall each one teach his neighbor and each his brother, saying, 'Know the LORD,' for they shall all know Me, from the least of them to the greatest, declares the LORD.

For I will forgive their iniquity, and I will remember their sin no more." (Jeremiah 31:33-34)

Glory to Glory Q&A

1. According to Ezekiel 11:17-20, why did the Lord promise to give the people a new heart and a new spirit?
2. What did Israel do that brought great shame and disrespect to the Lord's Name? (Ezekiel 36:16-38)
3. Which of the following statements did the Lord solemnly promise to do? (Jeremiah 31:33-34; Jeremiah 32:40-42)
   a. He will put His law in people's hearts.
   b. Everyone will know the Lord – from the least to the greatest.
   c. He will forgive their mistakes and no longer remember their sins.
   d. The Lord will not turn away from doing well to them.
   e. He will put the fear of the Lord in their hearts that they may not turn away from Him.
4. The Lord said that His people did things that had not even "come into His mind". What were the things they were doing? (See Jeremiah 7:31; 19:5 &32:35) How do you think it is possible for these things not to have entered His mind?
5. What gave Jeremiah hope in Lamentations 3:21-23?

Chapter 10

Job

Job 12:10
> In His hand are the life of every living thing and the breath of all mankind. (See also Acts 17:28)

The date for when Job lived is unknown, although Bible scholars date Job around the time of Abraham.

Having Conversations about God, or With God?

Satan had asked the Lord if he could test Job. When things were really hard for Job and he had lost everything, he and his friends had conversations about God. Obviously, the Lord knew everything that they were saying.

Then the Lord replied to Job and his friends' conversations about Him, revealing the splendor of His majesty in a face-to-face encounter with Job.

God's earnest desire is to have intimate conversations with you.

Jesus promised that "Those who love Me, will follow My instructions and I will manifest (reveal) Myself to him and We will come and make our home with him" (John 14:21&23).

This is the life you were meant to live: in union and companionship with the Lord. This is where you'll find fullness of joy – in that special place in the spirit where you fellowship with the Lord face-to-face.

Our "movie" will not be complete without including parts of God's conversation with Job. I highly recommend that you read the full conversation in Job 38-42.

Words Without Knowledge

Job 38:1-3
> Then the LORD answered Job out of the whirlwind and said: "Who is this that darkens counsel by words without knowledge? Dress for action like a man; I will question you, and you make it known to Me."

Where Were You…?

Job 38:4-13 (ISV)
> "Where were you when I laid the foundation of My earth? Tell Me, since you're so informed! Who set its measurement? Am I to assume you know? Who stretched a boundary line over it? On what were its bases set? Who laid its corner stone while the morning stars sang together and all the divine beings shouted joyfully?
>
> Who enclosed the sea with limits when it gushed out of the womb, when I made clouds to be its clothes and thick darkness its swaddling blanket, when I proscribed a boundary for it, set in place bars and doors for it; and said, 'You may come only this far and no more. Your majestic waves will stop here.'?
>
> Have you ever commanded the morning at any time during your life? Do you know where the dawn lives, where it seizes the edge of the earth and shakes the wicked out of it?"

Job 38:16-38 (ISV)
> "Have you been to the source of the sea and walked about in the recesses of the deepest ocean?
>
> Have the gates of death been revealed to you? Have you seen the gates of the deepest darkness?
>
> Do you understand the breadth of the earth? Tell me, since you know it all!
>
> Where is the road to where the light lives? Or where does the darkness live? Can you take it to its homeland, since you know the path to his house? You should know! After all, you had been born back then, so the number of your days is great!

Have you entered the storehouses of the snow or seen where the hail is stored, which I've reserved for the tribulation to come, for the day of battle and war?

Where is the lightning diffused or the east wind scattered around the earth?

Who cuts canals for storm floods, and paths for the lightning and thunder, to bring rain upon a land without inhabitants, a desert in which no human beings live, to satisfy a desolate and devastated desert, causing it to sprout vegetation?

Does the rain have a father? Who fathered the dew? Whose womb brings forth the ice? Who gives birth to frost out of an empty sky, when water solidifies like stone and the surface of the deepest sea freezes?

Can you bind the chains of Pleiades or loosen the cords of Orion?

Can you bring out constellations in their season? Can you guide the Bear with her cubs?

Do you know the laws of the heavens? Can you regulate their authority over the earth?

Can you call out to the clouds, so that abundant water drenches you? Can you command the lightning, so that it goes forth and calls to you, 'Look at us!'

Who sets wisdom within you, or imbues your mind with understanding? Who has the wisdom to be able to count the clouds, or to empty the water jars of heaven, when dust dries into a mass and then breaks apart into clods?"

Job 39:1-4 (ISV)
"Do you know when the mountain goat gives birth? Do you watch the doe as it calves its young? Can you count the months of their gestation? Do you know the time when they give birth, when they crouch down to give birth to their offspring, and let go of their birth pangs? Their young are strong; they grow up in the open field; then they go off and don't return to them."

Job 39:10-30 (ISV)
"Can you bind the ox to plow a furrow with a rope? Will he harrow after you in the valley? Will you trust him because of his great strength and entrust your labor to him? Will you trust him that he'll bring in your grain, and gather it to your threshing floor?

The wings of the ostrich flap joyously, but aren't its pinions and feathers like the stork?

She abandons her eggs on the ground and lets them be warmed in the sand, but she forgets that a foot might crush them or any wild animal might trample them.

She mistreats her young as though they're not hers, and she has no fear that her labor may be in vain, because God didn't grant her wisdom and never gave her understanding. And yet when she gets ready to run, she laughs at the horse and its rider.

Do you instill the horse with strength? Do you clothe its neck with a mane? Can you make him leap like the locust, and make the splendor of his snorting terrifying?

He paws the ground in the valley and rejoices in his strength; he goes out to face weapons. He scoffs at fear and is never scared; he never retreats from a sword. A quiver of arrows rattles against his side, along with a flashing spear and a lance.

Leaping in his excitement, he takes in the ground; he cannot stand still when the trumpets sound! When the trumpet blasts he'll neigh, 'Aha! Aha!' From a distance he can sense war, the war cry of generals, and their shouting.

Is it by your understanding that the hawk flies, spreading its wings toward the south? Does the eagle soar high at your command and build its nest on the highest crags?

He dwells on the crags where he makes his home, there on the rocky crag is his stronghold. From there he searches for prey, and his eyes recognize it from a distance.

His young ones feast on blood; he'll be found wherever there's a carcass."

Shall a Fault-finder Challenge the Almighty?

Job 40:1-2
    And the LORD said to Job: "Shall a faultfinder contend with the Almighty? He who argues with God, let him answer it."

Job 40:3-14
    Then Job answered the LORD and said:"Behold, I am of small account; what shall I answer You? I lay my hand on my mouth. I have spoken once, and I will not answer; twice, but I will proceed no further."

    Then the LORD answered Job out of the whirlwind and said: "Dress for action like a man; I will question you, and you make it known to Me. Will you even put Me in the wrong? Will you condemn Me that you may be in the right?

Have you an arm like God, and can you thunder with a voice like His? Adorn yourself with majesty and dignity; clothe yourself with glory and splendor. Pour out the overflowing of your anger, and look on everyone who is proud and abase him.

Look on everyone who is proud and bring him low and tread down the wicked where they stand. Hide them all in the dust together; bind their faces in the world below. Then will I also acknowledge to you that your own right hand can save you."

Job 41:1-8

"Can you draw out Leviathan with a fishhook or press down his tongue with a cord? Can you put a rope in his nose or pierce his jaw with a hook? Will he make many pleas to you?

Will he speak to you soft words? Will he make a covenant with you to take him for your servant forever? Will you play with him as with a bird, or will you put him on a leash for your girls?

Will traders bargain over him? Will they divide him up among the merchants? Can you fill his skin with harpoons or his head with fishing spears? Lay your hands on him; remember the battle – you will not do it again!"

Job 42:1-7

Then Job answered the LORD and said: "I know that You can do all things, and that no purpose of Yours can be thwarted.

'Who is this that hides counsel without knowledge?'

Therefore I have uttered what I did not understand, things too wonderful for me, which I did not know.

'Hear, and I will speak; I will question you, and make it known to me.'

I had heard of You by the hearing of the ear, but now my eye sees You; therefore I despise myself, and repent in dust and ashes."

After the LORD had spoken these words to Job, the LORD said to Eliphaz the Temanite: "My anger burns against you and against your two friends, for you have not spoken of Me what is right, as My servant Job has."

And the LORD restored the fortunes of Job when he had prayed for his friends. And the LORD gave Job twice as much as he had before (Job 42:10).

Glory to Glory Q&A

1. Is what you know about God based on what others have told you, or on having a personal relationship with Him?
2. What is the biggest revelation that you've ever had about God?
3. What would you like to tell an atheist, who arrogantly denies God's existence, and has made it a mission to not only make fun of Him, but also of those who believe in Him?
4. Now ask the Lord what He would like you to tell an atheist?

Chapter 11

The Remaining Books of the Old Testament

The period of the earthly kings of Judah and Israel has come to an end.

You will notice how there is a shift in the remainder of the prophetic books to prophesy not only about the events of the time, but to release decrees about the coming kingdom of Jesus Christ. The appointed time for God's Kingdom to be revealed was drawing closer!

Meanwhile, the remnant of the exiles was returning to Israel to rebuild what was destroyed.

Nahum (658 – 615 BC)

The Lord comforted Judah through the prophet Nahum saying, "Though I have afflicted you, I will afflict you no more. I will break this bond off you". (See Nahum 1:13)

Nahum 1:15 (GW)
> There on the mountains are the feet of a messenger who announces the good news: "All is well!" Celebrate your festivals, Judah! Keep your vows! This wickedness will never pass your way again. It will be completely removed.

The Lord also declared through Nahum the destruction of Nineveh, the capital city of Assyria and oppressors of Israel.

A Timeline From Around the Exile to the Birth of Jesus Christ

Prophets	Israel/Judah History	World and other leaders
Nahum (658-615) Jeremiah (650-582) Zephaniah (640-626) Ezekiel(620-570) Daniel (620-540) Habakkuk (608-598) Obadiah (590) Zechariah (522-509) Haggai (520) Malachi (465) Joel (450)	Temple and Jerusalem destroyed (586) Judah exiled to Babylon Gedaliah, governor of Judah (586) Ezra – Cyrus' sending Jews back (538) Rebuilding of temple in Jerusalem 536-516) Zerubbabel and Jeshua lead the Jews to finish the temple (520-516) Esther (478) Ezra sent to Judah (457) Nehemiah governs Judah (444-432) Nehemiah in Babylon (432-430) Palestine ruled by Egyptian Ptolemies (331-198BC), the Syrian Seleucides (198-163BC). Temple rededicated (Hanukkah 164 BC) Jewish Self-rule (164-63BC) Pompey conquers Jerusalem for Rome (63BC)	Nineveh, capital of Assyria falls to Persia and Medes (612) Nebuchadnezzar II (604-562) Darius (Gubaru) the Mede, governor of Babylon (539) Buddha, India (550-480) Cyrus the great (559-530) Confucius, China (551-479) Darius I (522-486) Xerxes I (Ahasuerus 485-465) Artaxerxes (464-424)

Daniel (620 – 540 BC)

Daniel, a contemporary prophet of Jeremiah and Ezekiel, was not a man of war, but a man of faith and principle. He valued what God valued.

He and his three friends had relentless trust, faithfulness, and obedience to the Lord. Do you remember the golden statue, the fiery furnace (Daniel 3), and the lion's den (Daniel 6)?

Their faith in God was absolutely unwavering and not once did God let them down, proving that He would not put anyone to shame who put their hope and trust in Him, doing what He said they should do.

They glorified God through their faith and absolute trust in Him.

Daniel was called upon a number of times to interpret the dreams of the kings of the day, for the Spirit of God gave him the interpretations.

King Nebuchadnezzar was humbled by the Lord and learned that the Most High rules the kingdom of men and gives it to which He will. He admitted and *"praised, extolled and honored the King of heaven, for all His works are right and His ways are just; and those who walk in pride, He is able to humble"* (Daniel 4:25, 37).

Daniel's Vision of the Four Beasts

Daniel 7:1-8 describes the vision that the Lord gave him, of four great beasts that came out of the sea.

The first beast was a lion that had eagles' wings. The wings were plucked off and he was made to stand on two feet like a man, and he was given the mind of a man.

The second beast was like a bear, raised up on one side, with three ribs in its mouth between its teeth. He was told to devour much flesh.

The third beast was like a leopard, with four wings of a bird on its back, and four heads, and dominion was given to it.

The fourth beast was exceedingly terrifying and strong. It had great iron teeth and devoured and broke everything into pieces, then stomped what was left with its feet. It was different from the other three beasts, and it had ten horns. Then another little horn came up after three of the first horns were plucked up by their roots. This horn had eyes like a man and a mouth speaking amazing things.

The Ancient of Days Reigns

Daniel 7:9-12

> As I looked, thrones were placed, and the Ancient of Days took His seat; His clothing was white as snow, and the hair of His head like pure wool; His throne was fiery flames; its wheels were burning fire.
>
> A stream of fire issued and came out from before Him; a thousand thousands served Him, and ten thousand times ten thousand stood before Him; the court sat in judgment, and the books were opened.
>
> I looked then because of the sound of the great words that the horn was speaking. And as I looked, the beast was killed, and its body destroyed and given over to be burned with fire. As for the rest of the beasts, their

dominion was taken away, but their lives were prolonged for a season and a time.

The Son of Man Is Given Dominion

Daniel 7:13-14
> "I saw in the night visions, and behold, with the clouds of heaven there came one like a son of man, and He came to the Ancient of Days and was presented before Him.
>
> <u>And to Him was given dominion and glory and a kingdom, that all peoples, nations, and languages should serve Him; His dominion is an everlasting dominion, which shall not pass away, and His kingdom one that shall not be destroyed.</u>

Daniel's Vision Interpreted

Daniel described his spirit as being anxious and he was alarmed by what he saw. Then he asked someone who stood there to explain the truth of what he had seen (Daniel 7:15-17).

So, he was told that the four great beasts were four kings who would arise out of the earth.

The Saints of the Most High Shall Receive and Possess the Kingdom Forever

Daniel 7:18
> <u>But the saints of the Most High shall receive the kingdom and possess the kingdom forever, forever and ever.</u>

Then Daniel wanted to know the truth about the fourth beast.

As he was looking, the horn that came up last made war with the saints until the "Ancient of Days came, and judgment was given for the saints of the Most High, and the time came when the saints possessed the kingdom (Daniel 7:19-22)."

Daniel 7:23-28
> Thus He said: "As for the fourth beast, there shall be a fourth kingdom on earth, which shall be different from all the kingdoms, and it shall devour the whole earth, and trample it down, and break it to pieces.
>
> As for the ten horns, out of this kingdom ten kings shall arise, and another shall arise after them; he shall be different from the former ones, and shall put down three kings.

He shall speak words against the Most High, and shall wear out the saints of the Most High, and shall think to change the times and the law; and they shall be given into his hand for a time, times, and half a time.

But the court shall sit in judgment, and his dominion shall be taken away, to be consumed and destroyed to the end.

And the kingdom and the dominion and the greatness of the kingdoms under the whole heaven shall be given to the people of the saints of the Most High; His kingdom shall be an everlasting kingdom, and all dominions shall serve and obey Him."

Here is the end of the matter. As for me, Daniel, my thoughts greatly alarmed me, and my colour changed, but I kept the matter in my heart.

Obadiah (590 BC)

The Kingdom of the Lord – Sowing and Reaping

Obadiah prophesied about the sowing and reaping principle of the kingdom of God.

Obadiah 1:15
> For the day of the LORD is near upon all the nations. As you have done, it shall be done to you; your deeds shall return on your own head.

The Promise That ALL the Nations Shall Drink Continually

Obadiah 1:16
> "For as you have drunk on My holy mountain, so all the nations shall drink continually; they shall drink and swallow, and shall be as though they had never been."

Habakkuk (608 – 598 BC)

The Righteous Shall Live by Faith

The Lord gave Habakkuk a vision, and told him to write it down, so *"he may RUN who reads it."*

For the vision awaited its appointed time, it hurries to the end and it will not lie. If it would seem slow, wait for it, for it will certainly come and not delay (Habakkuk 2:2-3).

Habakkuk 2:4 (ISV)
> "Notice their arrogance – they have no inward uprightness – but the righteous will live by their faith."

The Hebrew word for "faith" used here in Habakkuk 2:4, is "emunah" (Strongs H530), which means "firmness, security, stability, truth".

There are two parts in this verse. Either you put your faith in your own effort and in who you are, or you put your faith in God.

Faith by Submitting to Christ, Rather Than Your Flesh

What I believe the Lord is saying here is, "Be careful when your soul is puffed up and you consider yourself more important than is necessary, for you are opening yourself up to deception and wrongdoing.

It is better to submit yourself to the Lord and depend totally on Him to put you into right standing with Him and to put all of your trust and confidence in Him rather than in your own power. Then you will experience steadfast security in the Lord and be stable in all of your ways, because you rely only on Him."

The Earth Shall Be Filled With the Knowledge of the Glory of the Lord

Habakkuk 2:12-14 (ISV)
> "Woe to the one who founds a city upon bloodshed, and constructs a city by lawlessness.
>
> Is it not because of the LORD of the Heavenly Armies that people grow tired putting out fires, and nations weary themselves over nothing?
>
> Indeed, the earth will be filled with knowledge of the glory of the LORD, as water fills the sea."

Habakkuk Found His Joy in the Lord, Despite Rough Circumstances

Living a life of faith in the Lord is about much, much more than "getting stuff" from Him.

Living a life of faith in the Lord is when God Himself is enough for you. It is when you come to the realization that when you have God, you have all you will ever need and are content with that.

Habakkuk set an example of living a life of peaceful trust in God, by his following words:

Habakkuk 3:17-19 (ISV)
> Even though the fig tree does not blossom, and there are no grapes on the vines; even if the olive harvest fails, and the fields produce nothing edible; even if the flock is snatched from the sheepfold, and there is no

herd in the stalls – as for me, I will rejoice in the LORD. I will find my joy in the God who delivers me.

The LORD God is my strength – he will make my feet like those of a deer, equipping me to tread on my mountain heights.

Haggai (520 BC)

The Awesome Hope of the Latter Glory Being Greater!

Haggai 2:6-9 (ISV)
> For this is what the LORD of the Heavenly Armies says: "Once more, in a little while, I will make the heavens, the earth, the sea, and the dry land to shake.
>
> I will shake all nations, and the One desired by all nations will come. Then I will fill this house with glory," says the LORD of the Heavenly Armies.
>
> "The silver belongs to Me, as does the gold," declares the LORD of the Heavenly Armies.
>
> "The glory of this present house will be greater than was the former," declares the LORD of the Heavenly Armies. "And in this place I will grant peace," declares the LORD of the Heavenly Armies.

The glory of the New Covenant of the Spirit, written on human hearts, exceeds the glory of the former covenant written on tablets of stone! (2 Corinthians 3)

Under the new covenant, anyone in their ordinary, everyday life, may turn to the Lord and be transformed by His Spirit from one degree of glory to another.

Zechariah (522 – 509 BC)

Zechariah prophesied about the coming salvation of the Lord whereby many shall be joined and justified by Him!

Many Shall be Joined to the Lord and He Shall Live With Them

Zechariah 2:8-11 (GW)
> This is what the LORD of Armies says: Afterwards, the Glory sent Me to the nations who looted you. Whoever touches you touches the apple of His eye.

I'm going to shake My fist at the nations, and their own slaves will loot them. Then you will know that the LORD of Armies has sent Me.

Sing for joy and rejoice, people of Zion. I'm going to come and live among you, declares the LORD.

On that day many nations will join the LORD and become My people. I will live among you. Then you will know that the LORD of Armies has sent Me to you.

Trusted With Ministry, When Walking According to God's Rules

The angel of the Lord assured Joshua the high priest, in Zechariah 3:6-7:
"Thus says the LORD of hosts: If you will walk in My ways and keep My charge, then you shall rule My house and have charge of My courts, and I will give you the right of access among those who are standing here."

The Lord's Servant, the Branch

Zechariah 3:8-10
"Hear now, O Joshua the high priest, you and your friends who sit before you, for they are men who are a sign: behold, I will bring My servant the Branch.

For behold, on the stone that I have set before Joshua, on a single stone with seven eyes, I will engrave its inscription, declares the LORD of hosts, and I will remove the iniquity of this land in a single day.

In that day," declares the LORD of hosts, "every one of you will invite his neighbor to come under his vine and under his fig tree."

Ezra and Nehemiah (538 – 430 BC)

The humbled remnant of Jews returned to Jerusalem to rebuild the temple and the walls, as the Lord had promised.

The Lord worked in the hearts of the kings of Persia and organized circumstances to enable Nehemiah as governor, and also Ezra, the priest, to return to Jerusalem.

Nehemiah wept for the broken Jerusalem and worked with great dedication to govern the people to work together in families, everyone building in front of their own homes, to rebuild the walls of Jerusalem. The Lord protected them and provided for them.

Esther (478 BC)

Esther interceded for her people in the days of King Ahasuerus (Xerxes I, 478BC), who reigned from India to Ethiopia, over 127 provinces, whose throne was in Susa the citadel.

The book of Esther is another testimony of how God positions people and organizes circumstances to preserve and carry out His plans and His purposes.

When reading the events of Esther in the Spirit, I find it to be symbolic of Israel's rejection of the Lord, and the Lord's decision to choose for Himself a new bride...

Malachi (465 BC)

The Lord's Messenger (John the Baptist) to Prepare the Way

Malachi 3:1 (ISV)
"Watch out! I'm sending My messenger, and he will prepare the way before Me. Then suddenly the LORD you are looking for will come to His Temple. He is the messenger of the covenant whom you desire. Watch out! He is coming!" says the LORD of the Heavenly Armies.

Refiner and Purifier of Silver

Malachi 3:2-3
But who can endure the day of His coming, and who can stand when He appears? For He is like a refiner's fire and like fullers' soap.

He will sit as a refiner and purifier of silver, and He will purify the sons of Levi and refine them like gold and silver, and they will bring offerings in righteousness to the LORD.

Malachi 3:6-7
"For I the LORD do not change; therefore you, O children of Jacob, are not consumed.

From the days of your fathers you have turned aside from My statutes and have not kept them. Return to Me, and I will return to you, says the LORD of hosts. But you say, 'How shall we return?'"

Give to God What Belongs to God and He Will Bless You and Fight on Your Behalf

Malachi 3:8-12

> "Will man rob God? Yet you are robbing Me. But you say, 'How have we robbed you?' In your tithes and contributions. You are cursed with a curse, for you are robbing Me, the whole nation of you.
>
> Bring the full tithe into the storehouse, that there may be food in My house. And thereby put Me to the test, says the LORD of hosts, if I will not open the windows of heaven for you and pour down for you a blessing until there is no more need. I will rebuke the devourer for you, so that it will not destroy the fruits of your soil, and your vine in the field shall not fail to bear," says the LORD of hosts.
>
> "Then all nations will call you blessed, for you will be a land of delight," says the LORD of hosts.

To give to God is as old as mankind. Adam and Eve's children, Cain and Abel, gave offerings to God.

God accepted Abel's offering, because he offered to God out of **faith** (Hebrews 11:4). To give out of faith means to give up your own control and stubbornness, and to give your best from a pure heart simply because God asked you to give.

When you give to God by faith, you release into God's hands what you cannot achieve by yourself.

God wants to bless you and take care of you. Why not allow Him the privilege to do so?

The Great Day of the Lord

Malachi 4:1
> "For behold, the day is coming, burning like an oven, when all the arrogant and all evildoers will be stubble. The day that is coming shall set them ablaze," says the LORD of hosts, "so that it will leave them neither root nor branch."

The great day of the Lord is the resurrection power of Jesus Christ! After He triumphed over the enemy and death by dying on the cross, He took the keys of death from satan, to give **you** the authority to reign over sin and destruction in this life! (Luke 10:19, Romans 5:21 and Romans 6:12)

For You Who Respect and Honour My Name

Malachi 4:2-3
> But for you who fear My name, the sun of righteousness shall rise with healing in its wings. You shall go out leaping like calves from the stall.

And you shall tread down the wicked, for they will be ashes under the soles of your feet, on the day when I act, says the LORD of hosts.

For those who are led by the Holy Spirit will have the enemy under the soles of their feet and be empowered to not be ruled by their flesh (1 Corinthians 15:25, Revelation 5:10&11:15, Romans 8:14, Galatians 5:16-25).

Turning the Hearts to the Fathers

Malachi 4:4-6
> "Remember the law of My servant Moses, the statutes and rules that I commanded him at Horeb for all Israel. "Behold, I will send you Elijah the prophet before the great and awesome day of the LORD comes.
>
> And he will turn the hearts of fathers to their children and the hearts of children to their fathers, lest I come and strike the land with a decree of utter destruction.""

Jesus said that John the Baptist was Elijah who would come (Matthew 17:12, Mark 9:13).

Joel (450 BC)

Return to the Lord With All Your Heart

Joel 2:12-13
> "Yet even now," declares the LORD, "return to Me with all your heart, with fasting, with weeping, and with mourning; and rend your hearts and not your garments."
>
> Return to the LORD your God, for He is gracious and merciful, slow to anger, and abounding in steadfast love; and He relents over disaster.

The Lord's Promise to Pour Out His Spirit on ALL Flesh

Joel 2:28-31
> "And it shall come to pass afterward, that I will pour out My Spirit on all flesh; your sons and your daughters shall prophesy, your old men shall dream dreams, and your young men shall see visions. Even on the male and female servants in those days I will pour out My Spirit.
>
> And I will show wonders in the heavens and on the earth, blood and fire and columns of smoke. The sun shall be turned to darkness, and the moon to blood, before the great and awesome day of the LORD comes."

Everyone Who Calls on the Name of the Lord Shall Be Saved

Joel 2:32

And it shall come to pass that everyone who calls on the name of the LORD shall be saved. For in Mount Zion and in Jerusalem there shall be those who escape, as the LORD has said, and among the survivors shall be those whom the LORD calls.

God's Foundation Was Laid

We have come to the end of the Old Testament.

Through thousands of years, God has preserved and kept His Scriptures so that He can be made known to those He loves and deeply cares for.

In the Old Testament, God laid a foundation to make known His intentions, His heart, His ability and what He values most.

He laid this foundation, so that there will never again be any doubt about who He is, about what He can do, and about why He asks things and warns people. Those who know and are rooted in the Scriptures will be able to discern what is of God, and what is not, so that His Name will not be insulted or dishonoured anymore by people who are misrepresenting Him.

He also laid this foundation, so that people could have full confidence in Him and put their hope in His Word, His voice, and His promises – knowing that He watches over His Word to perform it (Jeremiah 1:12). He empowers them to persevere in faith, until they see the fulfillment of His promises. God is glorified and lifted high when He is proven faithful and honest.

The Old Testament created a standard by which to measure truth.

God hears the cry of the broken-hearted and He binds up their wounds. He looks at those who feel deep sorrow when they have done something wrong but are willing to change – allowing Him to circumcise their hearts when His ways are written there.

God didn't like hurt, pride, idolatry, sexual immorality, lying, cheating, exploitation of the poor, slander, greed, envy, giving false witness, and all the works of the flesh.

Disobedience, unbelief, stubbornness and rebellion against Him simply do not make sense to God as He knows that His intentions and ways are for the good of mankind and not for their harm.

He abhors oppression of any kind and He does not like it when He is misrepresented, or His character is dragged through the mud.

God has no pleasure in the death of anyone and would love for everyone to have a change of heart in order to do good rather than evil.

God does not meditate on evil, for He is holy and pure.

God always comes through for those who put their trust and confidence in Him, like He did for Abraham, Caleb, Rahab, and David, to name a few.

God loves when people ask for and follow His advice and help. He called it stupid when people didn't ask for, nor followed His advice or help.

The Promised Anointing: The "New" of God's Kingdom

It was prophesied that His messenger (John the Baptist) would be sent to prepare the way of the Lord.

God was about to establish the kingdom of the offspring of David (Jesus Christ), as an everlasting kingdom. His kingdom would fill the whole earth!

The Lord's anointed would be the good Shepherd who leads His flock, heals the broken-hearted and binds up their wounds. He would set the captives free and bring joy instead of mourning. He would restore sight to the blind and hearing to the deaf.

Upon Him would be the Spirit of wisdom and understanding, insight and knowledge, and the fear of the Lord.

He was about to take the punishment for the sins of the world, and He would bear the sorrows, transgressions, and iniquities of all, establishing the righteousness of God that believers could be justified by faith!

God's New Covenant would be established whereby He writes His laws on people's hearts and minds.

He was about to pour out His Spirit on all flesh for the sake of His holy name to empower people to do His will by giving them a new heart.

The righteous shall live by faith and the glory of the latter temple will be greater than the first.

The Lord promised peace and security, and to cleanse them from their guilt and sin.

He promised to raise up fishers of men. He advised when boasting to boast in the Lord.

He promised that He will gather His children from every nation and that the children of the barren (the Gentiles) will be many; she would call God her Maker and her Husband.

The Messiah would be a refiner like a purifier of silver. He would be born in Bethlehem and one day ride on a donkey.

They would cast lots over His garments.

By His offering for sins, He shall make many righteous and secure their inheritance to be obtained by God's grace for God's glory, and not by works of the flesh.

 Glory to Glory Q&A

Make a list of everything that you would like to thank and praise God for in your own life.

Chapter 12

God's Kingdom

The Time Has Come!

Mark 1:15 (GW)
   He (John the Baptist) said, "The time has come, and the kingdom of God is near. Change the way you think and act, and believe the Good News."

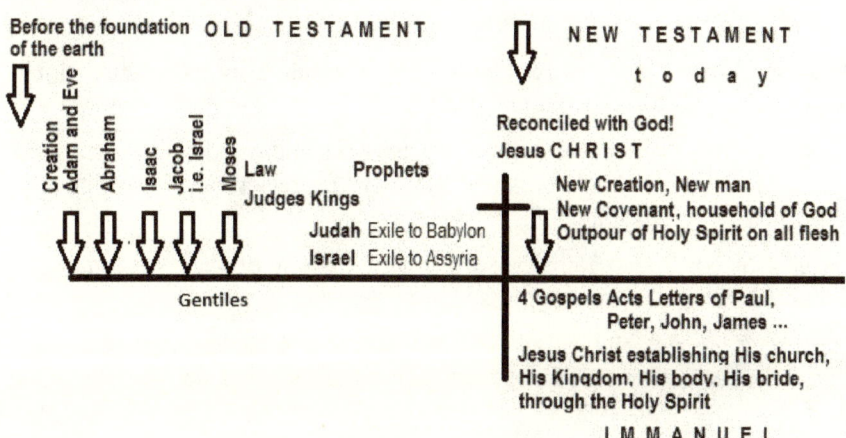

I love watching people and figuring out what makes them tick.

The first thing that the Holy Spirit told me to do after I was born again was to read the book of Luke. I wanted to know Jesus and I wanted to love Him. At that time, I knew that I didn't love Him, or knew Him, but I wanted to.

I was more interested in what He was doing than about what He was saying, because I felt that people's actions speak louder than words.

Needless to say – Jesus delivered on every level. He was everything that I ever wanted God to be, and more.

Wouldn't you agree that who God is, inspires one to do anything for Him?

Jesus

When you see Jesus, you've seen God.

Colossians 1:15-20 (GW)
> He is the image of the invisible God, the firstborn of all creation.
>
> He created all things in heaven and on earth, visible and invisible. Whether they are kings or lords, rulers or powers- everything has been created through Him and for Him.
>
> He existed before everything and holds everything together.
>
> He is also the head of the church, which is His body. He is the beginning, the first to come back to life so that He would have first place in everything.
>
> God was pleased to have all of Himself live in Christ.
>
> God was also pleased to bring everything on earth and in heaven back to Himself through Christ. He did this by making peace through Christ's blood sacrificed on the cross.

Jesus presented God's glory. God's glory was alive in every fibre of His being as He followed the Father's lead.

He showed God's ability and power by the signs and wonders He performed, and God's heart by His words and the way He treated people. (John 2:11, 4:48, 11:25-27, 40&John14:7, 10-14)

Jesus showed God's authority over the kingdom of darkness when He delivered many who were oppressed or possessed.

He healed the sick and raised the dead, because He is the resurrection and life. He made the lame walk, opened the eyes of the blind, and the ears of the deaf.

Everything that was prophesied about the Messiah, God's anointed, the Branch, the Christ, the shepherd, was made visible so that people could **believe** and be saved from death and sin (John 20:30-31)!

He came to conquer death and to give eternal life to all who believe in Him! He was outspoken about hypocrisy, oppression, and wrongdoing and taught to bless, do good, not judge, to pray, show mercy and love as our heavenly Father does (Matthew 5:38-48).

He lived the way, the truth, and the life.

The Tender Love and Mercy of God

The Bible declares over and over how God's heart is for the poor, the meek, the fatherless, the humble, the broken-hearted, the wounded, the hurt, the lost, the sensitive, the grieved, the disappointed, the frustrated, the rejected, and those with a remorseful and teachable heart and spirit – to bind up their wounds, to set them free, and to give them a home, a place to belong where they are safe, secure and loved.

Jesus' behavior gave evidence of the same love and compassion He had of Father God:

Luke 4:40-41
> Now when the sun was setting, all those who had any who were sick with various diseases brought them to Him, and He laid hands on every one of them and healed them.
>
> And demons also came out of many, crying, "You are the Son of God!" But He rebuked them and would not allow them to speak, because they knew that He was the Christ.

A Home and a Place to Belong Where All Nations Are Welcome

He came to give a home to the poor, the lost, and the fatherless.

Whoever believes in Jesus is given the right to become a child of God (John 1:12-13) and become part of God's household (Ephesians 1:5, 2:11-22).

In Christ, the division between Jews and Gentiles is removed, as all nations are welcome in God's spiritual home. There is room for everyone, fulfilling God's promise to Abraham and the words spoken by the prophets.

In Christ, there is no more racial or gender discrimination (Galatians 3:28-29).

The Lord assembles His children from every tongue, tribe and nation – as was prophesied by His prophets. He performs the miracle to make them born again, opening the eyes of their hearts to see Him, and to have certainty that they are His children.

By Jesus' offering on the cross, and His resurrection, He has opened up the heavens and the throne room of God, that you may be where He is and you may be joint heir of God.

Before being taken captive, Jesus prayed that all who believe will be in union with God, in the same way as the Father is in Him and He is in the Father (John 17:20-24). This is what Immanuel is - God with you every day of your life.

Upset at Hypocrisy, Oppression, Lying and Cheating

Jesus was upset at the hypocrisy of those who cleaned only the outside of the cup but failed to clean the inside. He was upset by leaders of the day who were oppressing His people, or leading them astray by lying, cheating, and making up things based on their traditions, and not on God (Matthew 21:28-46, 22:1-14, Matthew 23, Mark 7:6-13).

God's values and what He holds dear hasn't changed. The only thing that has changed is that God gave His Son so that all who do evil, and all who do not do evil, may be saved by God's grace.

Freed Through Faith

Salvation is a gift of God to all who believe. It is not because of the works of anyone so that no one could boast. When boasting, boast in God's incredible love and His merciful grace (Ephesians 2:8).

What was impossible in the Old Testament has been made possible from the New Testament onwards because of Jesus. By Him, everyone who believes is freed from everything that they couldn't be freed from by the law of Moses (Acts 13:38-39).

The focus of the law was sin. Without the law, people didn't know the difference between right and wrong (Romans 3:20; Galatians 3:19-22).

Jesus is God's solution to sin and wrongdoing, because He took the punishment for sin to restore people's hope that they are good enough for God.

What the law couldn't do was to empower people to overcome their sin.

Now, through faith in Jesus, anyone who is born of God has God in them and they are in God – all day and every day.

Whoever is born of God overcomes the world and the victory that overcomes the world is our faith (1 John 5:4).

This faith is to be absolutely certain that God is with you, His grace is enough for you, and He is able to help you with anything and everything.

Jesus Did God's will

Jesus was totally committed to doing Father God's will to establish His solution in the earth: to save people and help them live life from the Spirit, in union with God – both now and forever.

John 6:38-40
> For I have come down from heaven, not to do My own will but the will of Him who sent Me.
>
> And this is the will of Him who sent Me, that I should lose nothing of all that He has given Me, but raise it up on the last day.
>
> For this is the will of My Father, that everyone who looks on the Son and believes in Him should have eternal life, and I will raise him up on the last day."

For it is the Father's will that all come to repentance – to turn to Him, and to know life and not perish (2 Peter 3:9)!

Jesus, as the good Shepherd, earnestly assures everyone that nothing will be able to snatch His sheep out of His hand, nor out of His Father's hand. For the Father is greater than all and loves everyone.

Driven by the love for the Father and love for people, Jesus laid down His life of His own accord to save them, knowing that it was the Father's will (John 10:17-18&28-30, Isaiah 53:10-12).

The Great Commission

Before ascending into heaven, Jesus gave instruction to His disciples to go into the entire world and make disciples (students of Jesus Christ) of all nations, teaching them to hold dear everything that He had instructed them. He promised to be with them until the end of the age (Matthew 28:16-20).

This commission was passed down from generation to generation of believers over thousands of years.

At Pentecost, the Holy Spirit was poured out as promised, and they received the power of God to be His witnesses. Peter, John, James, Phillip and others were fearless in their faith and commitment to what they knew to be true. Yes, they each had their own journey, strengths and weaknesses, but Jesus was with them through His indwelling Spirit, guiding them, helping them, teaching them and reminding them of what He taught them everywhere they went.

Jesus called Paul as an apostle and revealed a great many things to him so that he could write most of what is known as the New Testament. The resurrected Jesus, seated at the right hand of God (1 John 2:1-2), was teaching Paul and telling him what to write (Galatians 1:10, 12& 2:1-2).

No man could have assembled the Bible as we have it today, without the power of God through the Holy Spirit. There are numerous versions and one is advised to compare them, but you will find that God is still God in any language or authentic version of the Bible, given as a Manual to ultimately equip anyone for living everyday life in faith and in a personal relationship with God.

It is the will of God that Christ be all in all – having His glory (God's ways and character) written on every heart and mind as God has sworn by His new covenant that was sealed by the blood of Jesus (Hebrews 8-10, Ephesians 1).

Jesus' Bride

Jesus Christ loves His bride, the Church, as a husband loves his wife (Ephesians 5:23-27) – and more.

He is the King of glory who lives in high places and also with those who are of a humble heart and a broken, teachable and remorseful spirit - His bride.

The first time that the word "church" is used in the Bible, is where Jesus declared that, "on this rock I will build My church and the gates of hell will not triumph over it" (Matthew 16:18).

I have to say it – it is sexy when a man protects his wife and declares his authority as he wants to help her grow, develop and rise up far above anything that wants to destroy her! This is what Jesus does and wants for His bride!

The word "church" in Greek means the "called out" ones.

So, if you've been wondering whether you are one of the called ones… well, if you're part of Jesus' church - then you are called! As one who is called, you were predestined by God, foreknown by Him, justified (washed in the blood) and glorified (seated with Christ in heavenly places)! You have been blessed with every spiritual blessing in the heavenly realm (Ephesians 1:3).

"Church" is used many times in the book of Acts and the letters of the apostles, as the early believers gathered in groups to fellowship, to receive teaching in the Word, to worship God, and to support one another. Together they had faith.

Acts 9:31

So the church throughout all Judea and Galilee and Samaria had peace and was being built up. And walking in the fear of the Lord and in the comfort of the Holy Spirit, it multiplied.

Still today, the letters of the apostles teach and train the churches (the groups of believers) to live the life of God's Kingdom, full of love and grace, as led by the Holy Spirit.

The apostle Paul wrote that he considered anything and everything as worthless because of the surpassing value of knowing Jesus Christ as Lord (Philippians 3:7-11).

Seated at the Right Hand of God

John describes what happened when he saw the risen and glorified Jesus in the vision he had on the way to Patmos, in Revelation 1:17-19:

> When I saw Him, I fell at His feet as though dead. But He laid his right hand on me, saying, "Fear not, I am the first and the last, and the living One. I died, and behold I am alive forevermore and I have the keys of Death and Hades. Write therefore the things that you have seen, <u>those that are</u> and <u>those that are to take place after this</u>.

He saw Jesus standing in the midst of the seven lamp stands, which symbolized the seven churches in Asia. Jesus dictated to John a message to be written to each of the churches.

Here are a few main things that He told the churches:

Encouragement

Jesus praised the love and service in many churches. He encouraged those who were persevering in faith in Him. He was pleased with those who continued with patient endurance to lift up His name and did not pursue evil.

Your First Love

Jesus sincerely asked them to not forget their first love – the passion they had for the Lord when they started their walk with Him.

Make it your first priority to live daily in a personal relationship with the Lord. If you feel offended by Him in any way, make it your mission to clean out your heart and your mind, and to reconnect with Him as His heart's desire is to pour out His love to you and to take care of you.

He loves you as much as He loved Israel and you've read how His passion is to fight for His beloved.

Check What You Believe

Some of the churches in Asia were following heresies and were pursuing gain from wrongdoing or were busy with the deep things of satan… things that Jesus did not approve of, and He earnestly advised those churches to correct those things (Revelations 2:6&2:14-15,24).

Check your doctrines. Be willing to surrender what you believe in your heart to be true, to Jesus, to be tested by His fire. What have you got to lose?

Flee From Sexual Immorality

Jesus didn't like that some churches were tolerating sexual immorality and adultery, without correction so that they may change their ways (Revelations 2:19-23&14).

Turn away from sexual immorality. It is not that God wants to "spoil your fun!" God invented sex, as He declared to Adam and Eve, husband and wife, "Be fruitful, multiply, and fill the earth!"

Paul advised the Church that those who are burning with sexual desire should marry. A marriage between a husband and wife is a beautiful Godly institution. They are meant to enjoy each other in body, soul, and in spirit. Have grace with each other as both grow and develop from glory to glory, learning to live in God's way of love. As Jesus said, "From the beginning God made man and woman to be husband and wife" (1 Corinthians 7:2&Matthew 19:3-9).

Be on Fire, Not Lukewarm

Do not think you are rich, not realizing that you are pitiable, poor, and blind – being neither hot nor cold (Revelation 3:1-3).

Allow the fire of Jesus to burn away the lethargy and anoint you with new spiritual vision to see. Let Him clothe you with His salvation to cover your shame.

He is standing at the door and He is knocking. Would you dine with Him?

Stand Firm in Faith and Endurance

Remain steadfast in faith and endurance during times of testing and difficult tribulations (Revelation 2:9-10, 13&3:10) for Jesus will reward you.

Do not shrink back when you feel challenged or confronted but grab a hold of God's hand and do not let go.

Hold Firmly

Hold firmly onto His Word and what He has given you (Revelations 2:2, 25-26&3:11, 18).

Do Not Say "I Need Nothing"

Revelation 3:17-19

> For you say, I am rich, I have prospered, and I need nothing, not realizing that you are wretched, pitiable, poor, blind, and naked.
>
> I counsel you to buy from Me gold refined by fire, so that you may be rich, and white garments so that you may clothe yourself and the shame of your nakedness may not be seen, and salve to anoint your eyes, so that you may see.
>
> Those whom I love, I reprove and discipline, so be zealous and repent.

In everything, turn to Jesus and let Him show you the next step.

 Glory to Glory Q&A

1. List 10 (or more) prophecies of the Messiah that were fulfilled by Jesus Christ.
2. Name one thing that you love the most about Jesus.

Part 3

How to Reign with Christ in Ordinary, Everyday Life

Chapter 13

Doing Life With God

In this book you find many ingredients that you can apply to your own life and journey with the Lord. I even threw in a recipe or two.

But, at the end of the day, it is up to you to use it, and apply it as you feel led to.

It is time for the final touches and to make sure that you are equipped and encouraged to live your own everyday life using God as your Manual and as your primary go-to Person.

Feed on Jesus

John 6:57
> As the living Father sent Me, and I live because of the Father, so whoever feeds on Me, he also will live because of Me.

It is impossible to do life without Jesus.

God's Vineyard

In the book of Isaiah, God called Israel His vineyard and He felt wounded when they didn't bear good fruit.

Today, all who believe in Jesus are part of God's vineyard.

Jesus said that He is the vine and we are the branches. If we remain in Him, and He in us, we will bear much fruit whereby Father God is glorified (John 15).

He is not only meant to live side by side with you, but to penetrate the deepest parts of your soul and be one with you. Without Jesus, you can't do anything.

When Your Life Crashes

Sometimes it happens that you know that you are a child of God, Spirit filled with access to the throne room, but then things go wrong, and it feels as if your life is crashing all around you. You want to shout, "Lord, what is happening?! I can't do this!"

What happened? Why did your life come crashing down?

For any and every question: Feed on Jesus. He will give you the faith, the direction and the answers you need.

Feed on the Word, and feed on truth. If you don't, the enemy will be only too happy to fill your head with lies and deceit to get you off track. If you search for answers outside of Christ, you are walking in dangerous territory. Don't turn to Tarot cards, witchcraft, astrology, speaking to the dead, or any other thing of the occult or what the Lord called "things of the east". They cannot help you! The devil comes like an angel of light and he likes to mess with your head and your heart.

Jesus' Triumph Is Yours

Jesus triumphed over the enemy when He died on the cross and took the keys of death from satan. Then, Jesus rose victoriously from the dead!

Now <u>you</u> need to sustain that victory in your own life by putting satan under your feet and God on the throne of your heart!

The same Spirit that rose Jesus from the dead lives **<u>in you</u>**. You can do this!

Esther

In the testimony of Esther, after the evil Haman was hanged, there remained one problem:

Before Haman died, he tricked King Ahashuerus to give him his signet ring that he used to send out letters to all provinces with instructions to kill, destroy and annihilate all Jews, young and old, and to plunder their goods. Because it was sealed with the king's ring it couldn't be revoked.

Fortunately, the king gave Esther his signet ring and new letters (sealed with the king's ring) were sent out: The Jews could defend themselves and struck all their enemies with the **sword** (Esther 9:5)!!!

The Sword of the Spirit

The Word of God is the sword of the Spirit (Ephesians 6:17).

Using God's truth from His Word together with the indwelling power of the Holy Spirit is pretty powerful, don't you think so?

There is a lot of knowledge in the world – a lot.

But there is one truth, one way to life – Jesus Christ (John 14:6). You either believe it or you don't. You cannot believe halfway.

There is one Father, one Holy Spirit, and one faith (Ephesians 4:4-6).

God created you and God can fix you if you need fixing. That's the bottom line.

The Genuineness of Your Faith

The Word says that you are to count it all joy when trials and tribulations come your way - why?

It is so that the genuineness of your faith can be tried and tested. At the same time, being under the pressure of trials, your perseverance and endurance are also developed (James 1:2-3 & 1 Peter 1:7-9).

You see, when all goes well, it is very easy to say that you believe. It is very easy to quote scripture and to preach and teach using a lot of words… but it is a whole different ball game to walk the talk when circumstances are tough.

It is during challenging storms that we are more inclined to ask:

- "Where was God?"
- "Where is God?"
- "Who is God?"
- "What do I really believe?"
- "Who can I trust?"
- "Where does my help come from?"
- "Where did I miss it? Did I miss it?"

King David faced many, many trials and tribulations, but he didn't let them define him. Instead, he sought God's face – he sought God's truth and he dug deep to do God's will. He meditated on God's word, saying that it was a lamp for his feet and a light for his path. Yeah, he made a few mistakes, but he took ownership of his mistakes and worked through his mistakes with his personal relationship with the Lord (Psalm 51).

God is able to let all things work together for good for those who have been called by His design and purpose.

You've seen how Moses, Abraham, David, Jonah, Joseph, Esther, Ruth and everyone else's lives all made sense because He made everything work together for good. He is doing so for you also. At this very moment, God is at work in your life and He knows every detail because He loves you. He wants to help you, and He wants you to excel and push through until you experience victory.

With the same comfort that God, the Father of all comfort, comforts you with during difficult times and afflictions, you will be able to comfort others (2 Corinthians 1:3-6).

See your challenges as training to equip you to help others. It's better to give what you've lived, for then it carries God's anointing: God writes His ways in hearts and minds and that is what you are called to impart to others.

So, embrace the pressures that are meant to renew you and equip you. These pressures will bring to light what is in your heart and mind, as well as what you truly believe, so that your faith is refined, by growing deeper and more genuine.

Supplement Your Faith

God Has Given You All You Need

Peter wrote that God has given you ALL things that pertain to life and godliness so that you may become a partaker of the divine nature (2 Peter 1:3-4)!

Your Main Purpose

This is your main purpose: to live God's way of life in companionship with Him.

God Trains You to Be Effective

For this reason (to live God's way of life in companionship with Him), Peter advised that you make every effort to supplement your faith with the qualities of virtue, knowledge, self-control, steadfastness, godliness, brotherly affection and love.

He said that if you practice those qualities, you will never fail, be ineffective or unfruitful! (2 Peter 1:5-15)

Knowledge of God

This book has been carefully put together to connect you with God's heart that you may know beyond a shadow of a doubt that you can trust Him.

Pursue excellence in knowing God more. Nothing else in the whole universe is more important than knowing God, because if you don't know Him, then your life has absolutely no meaning. For He is your Maker and you need to know what He made you for.

Virtue

Virtue is about God's ways and what He loves. Virtue rubs off on you the more time you spend with Him and in His Word.

Godliness: Self-control, Steadfastness and Love

Self-control, steadfastness and love are all fruit of the Spirit.

As you live your life led by the Holy Spirit, He will transform you from the inside out, causing you to bear His fruit.

He is the trainer in godliness as He writes the ways of Christ on your heart and mind when He trains you to know God's voice – throughout any trials, tribulations, crashes, mistakes, and victories.

God trains you in brotherly love and affection through relationships that He allows in your life. Through these relationships, you learn to love God's way. You learn not to think about yourself more than others or to insist on your own way and also not be arrogant or resentful but to endure all things (1 Corinthians 13).

LAUGH

LAUGH is an acronym that the Lord gave me. It summarizes the principles He has equipped me with over the years. I use it every day of my life and also when performing counseling.

LAUGH is a fun and quick way to assess yourself where you're at in your journey of doing life with the Lord.

L: Listen

What Do You Listen To?

We have seen that faith comes through hearing. So, what are you allowing into your heart and mind to influence you?

Take a moment to think about <u>yesterday</u> and answer the following questions–

- What or who did you listen to?
- What thoughts were going through your mind?
- What or who did you allow in your head and your heart to shape your thinking and your behavior?
- Who or what influenced your decisions and the choices you made?
- What or who did you give power to influence your faith?
- What or who did you place your hopes on?

A: Adore

What or Who Do You Adore?

Think about right now, <u>today</u>, while answering the following –

- What or who consumes your thoughts?
- What or who takes priority in your life?
- What or who will you always make time for?
- What or who will you always have money for?

What consumes you will have control over you.

U: Uncomplicate

- What drives you?
- What haunts you?
- Is there anybody that you need to forgive?
- Do you have absolute peace and joy in your heart and soul?
- Who do you blame for your problems?
- Is there anything that is not of God in your heart that you need to let go of?

Things that are not of Christ will complicate your life.

Things like feelings of inferiority, rejection, adultery, sexual immorality, strife, a relentless desire to keep up with the Jones', envy, fear, guilt, shame, disappointments, abnormal grief and sorrow.

Emotional stress is very draining. What is giving you emotional stress right now? About the things that are giving you stress, what is in your control and what not?

While reading this book, you might have been confronted with a judgmental and vengeful Jonah in you; or, an unbelieving Saul who followed his own mind and went off to consult a medium and did witchcraft; perhaps a disobedient Solomon who ignored his father's (as well as the Lord's) advice

– with dire consequences; or, a stubborn, rebellious, and proud Israel who were opposing and rejecting the Lord as many didn't seek to follow His voice, but used fortune telling, idolatry or traditions that they picked up from unbelievers.

What are you secretly busy with that is not of the Lord? Or, have you perhaps felt convicted when reading about the false prophets, who copied the words of others or who prophesied to receive acceptance and approval from people, rather than making sure that you are speaking what God wants to say?

Jesus

Jesus' forgiveness and grace has the power to uncomplicate your life by washing you clean with His blood. Why not give Him anything and everything that you've been struggling to "fix" on your own?

He can do what you cannot do. Let go of the things that you have absolutely no control over.

It's no use crying over spilt milk either.

Simply walk with Jesus by the power of the Holy Spirit as He trains you and teaches you to live the life that God intended for your life.

Psalms 86:11
> Teach me Your way, O LORD, that I may walk in Your truth; unite my heart to fear Your name.

The Lord keeps in perfect peace those whose minds are set on Him (Isaiah 26:3-4). It is a promise of God. It is part of your inheritance. Take it.

Whatever is pure, whatever is lovely, whatever is true – think about these things and your peace will be great (Philippians 4:8-9).

Uncomplicate your life by having the peace of Christ rule in your heart by following His advice.

G: Grounded

Grounded is to be sensible and well balanced; to be rooted in Christ and have peace with who you are.

What is Your Spiritual House Built On?

Take a moment to answer these questions honestly –

- Are you truly grounded in the Word?
- Are you easily persuaded or confused with different doctrines, religions and ideas – or do you have firm convictions, rooted in Jesus Christ?

- Do you have a personal relationship with the Lord?
- Do you hear God's voice?
- Are you happy with whom God made you to be?
- List your spiritual gifts, natural talents, your strengths and weaknesses. Are you happy with whom you are?
- Do you know what God has called you for?
- Do you know who you are?

H: Habit

What or Who Has Power Over You?

- What healthy habits do you have that energize you and give you great joy and peace?
- Do you perhaps have an unhealthy habit that is controlling your mind, your heart or your behavior? A habit that is destroying your finances, your relationships and/or your peace of mind?

Hopefully, while reading, you've picked up a few healthy habits from David, Jesus, and others who were led by the Spirit as you saw the outcome of their choices, faith, and obedience.

Transformation

Transformation happens when you put off the old and put on Christ (Ephesians 4:17-32 & Colossians 3).

Gold

When God wants to transform you, He is NOT saying that you are not good enough! In fact, He is saying that you ARE worthy. You are more precious than gold.

Because gold is precious, it goes through fire so that the dross is removed and only the pure gold remains.

You are a child of God – born from above. You are a new creation. Christ lives in you – it is who you are (2 Corinthians 5:17; Ephesians 1:5, 23&3:17).

Does your behavior reflect who God made you to be? Yes, we have the treasure of Christ in jars of clay so that the magnificent power and the glory belong to God and not to us.

When you are under pressure, what comes out? Does Christ come out, or your flesh? What is in you that is not of Christ?

When you feel that pressure, allow that fleshy thing to be exposed and give it to Jesus, so that Christ takes its place in your heart and the life of Jesus may be manifested in your mortal body (2 Corinthians 4:7-18).

Grace is Your Trainer

Titus 2:11-12
> For the **grace** of God has appeared, bringing salvation to all people, **training** us to renounce ungodliness and worldly passions, and to live self-controlled, upright, and godly lives in the present age

Every time you mess up, God's grace is there to comfort, encourage and heal you so that you can grow. Jesus is with you every step of your journey. God's grace is your safety net to help you develop through to spiritual maturity.

God's grace is **ointment** poured out on a wounded soul, encouraging you to let go of the old and to embrace the new.

He knows what He has put in you and predestined you for.

Why not let Him develop your full potential?

 ## Glory to Glory Q&A

Please answer the LAUGH questions if you have not done so already.

Chapter 14

Training in Virtue

Being Genuine

Romans 12:9
> Let love be genuine. Abhor what is evil; hold fast to what is good.

Have you ever tried to be good and to do good all the time?

It's hard, isn't it?

That is why God's grace is your trainer and your safety net.

It is not a matter of being good all the time, but it's about having the **desire** in your heart to do what is good and to be what is good.

Is your love genuine?

Your habits have power to define who you are and what you do, because they condition you into a way of life which is either good or bad for you. Sometimes people have good habits, and sometimes they have learned a few bad habits in order to "cope" with "life".

In Christ, you are a brand new creation (2 Corinthians 5:17).

It's time to claim back the new in your heart and your soul if, maybe, it got buried under some unhealthy stuff somewhere along your life journey.

It's time to be genuine again.

As a Child

Jesus said:

Mark 10:15
> Truly, I say to you, whoever does not receive the kingdom of God like a child shall not enter it."

Wounds of the past could have conditioned you to be "strong" and "fierce" when you are not. It's okay to be weak and vulnerable like a small child, because you have a God who wants to fight for you.

I'd like to challenge you to unlearn a few bad habits that have unnecessarily complicated your life.

1. Trust God Like a Little Child

A child does not worry about the parents' budget. Children simply trust that they will be fed, clothed, and have a place to live. Children have unwavering faith in their parents' abilities.

Every child yearns for a parent whom they can trust, who gives them a home where they are safe and protected and where they are taught to live a good life.

When Jesus was arrested, and someone drew a sword to defend them, He confidently exclaimed, "Do you think I cannot appeal to My Father and He will at once send Me more than twelve legions of angels?"

Jesus had child-like confidence, because He knew His Father. He also knew for certain what Father God had told Him to say and shown Him what to do.

John 13:3-5 (ISV)
> Because Jesus **knew** that the Father had given everything into His control, that He had come from God, and that He was returning to God, therefore He got up from the table, removed His outer robe, and took a towel and fastened it around His waist.
>
> Then He poured some water into a basin and began to wash the disciples' feet and to dry them with the towel that was tied around His waist.

Jesus was perfectly secure in His relationship with the Father, which made Him feel secure in Himself, His identity and purpose.

You Are Safe

Receiving the kingdom as a child places you in a position of safety and security in closeness with the Father. He teaches you who you are, where you fit in, and trains you what to do.

When you are secure in whom God has made you to be, you are able to serve others through loving them.

2. Be as Sincere as a Small Child

A child cannot fake compassion and love. That is what makes them so vulnerable to abuse and to be tricked into doing stuff that they were never meant (or created) to be doing.

Jesus had sincere compassion for the broken, the hurt, the poor, the sick, and those in captivity. He didn't fake it. When a leper asked Him if He wanted to heal him, Jesus was filled with compassion, and even touched him and said, "I will. Be clean."

Consider that under the law, Jesus wasn't meant to touch the leper for he was unclean. Jesus sincerely felt compassion for the guy! (Mark 1:40-45)

Jesus was consumed with zeal for the house of the Lord, because of their greed, lying, cheating, and planning of schemes to oppress and manipulate those who, with their best intentions, tried to serve God.

Restore Your Innocence

When you've lost your innocence, and have built walls to protect yourself, you need to regain your trust in God, to allow Him to come inside your walls to bring the healing. Once He has healed you, and Christ gives you the strength to be vulnerable and to love again, God can be your shield, your fortress, your safe place, and protector.

If Jesus was moved with compassion for the leper, don't you think that He has heard your cries and seen your deepest sorrow and wants to help you? If Jesus didn't think twice before touching a leper, do you honestly think that any mistake that you have ever made would put Him off from wanting to touch you?

I daresay, if you asked Him today, "Jesus, if You will, make me clean," He will.

Have Mercy

Furthermore, it's good to remember that everyone needs God. Any mistakes that you, your parents, your friends, your spouse, and others in your life have made serve as a reminder to worship only God, and not any idol-like image made of any person or entity.

I see mistakes and weaknesses in people and in myself, as reminders to have mercy and grace with one another, just like God has with you and me.

If God could forgive, why not us? We are not God. Let God be God – and God chose to give His everything that all would have a chance to be saved when they accept His love.

Let us therefore pursue to be imitators of God. Forgive and bless those who cursed you, insulted you or did you harm, just like God did.

3. Be as Honest as a Small Child

Many years ago, I attended a women's camp where I heard a lady telling us about an incident she had experienced with her granddaughter. She said that while she was putting moisturizer and night cream onto her face, her granddaughter asked her what she was doing. So, she said that she was putting on cream and moisturizer to prevent wrinkles. The little girl stared at her for a moment, and then exclaimed, "But Granny... it's not working!"

That is the pure honesty of a child.

When they don't like a gift, they'll tell you. If the gift is broken, they'll tell you.

Please don't be all religious with God. He can see through all the falseness and the lies. Tell Him when you are not happy and when your stuff is broken and ask Him to please help you fix it.

Often the problem is not that the gift is broken, but that they don't know how to use it. They might need to read the manual and follow the instructions, or ask their father, mother, brother, or sister to teach them to use the gift.

The night in Gethsemane Jesus was pouring out His heart to His Father in all honesty, asking Him if it was at all possible for Him to remove the cup that He was about to drink, He simply exposed His true feelings and emotions to His Father, and Father God gave Him the strength to push through.

Become a Child Again

What are you battling with at the moment? What is broken in your life? God is with you right now, ready to listen.

Reclaim your childlike honesty and purity and get any lies out of your system. Check anything and everything that you are doing secretly – how are they serving you?

Ask yourself what needs these secret actions are fulfilling in your life. How, do you think God would want to fulfill those needs?

Fundamentally, all your basic needs should be fulfilled by God: your needs for security, provision, love, acceptance, comfort, recognition, to be fed, and to receive direction.

4. Use Gifts as Enthusiastically as a Small Child

Have you ever seen a child play with a gift that they have just received? They go at it with everything they've got! They go at it with wholehearted enthusiasm and joy!

Have you ever seen children on a treasure hunt? They bounce around with excitement and cannot wait for the clues to be read! Then they fervently search for the treasure, and run between treasure points, thrilled by the excitement to hunt for something that they have not seen yet.

Jesus said that the kingdom of heaven is like a treasure hidden in a field. You need to find that treasure! There is kingdom-treasure inside you, inside others, and inside the Word! There are things there you haven't seen yet!

No matter the cost, no matter the effort, don't stop until you know you have found what you were meant to find. In finding it, you will know, and you will experience such peace and joy that goes far above and beyond the peace and joy that the world can give!

Jesus loved so much to be able to heal the sick that He did it through the night!

To be able to bring kingdom-healing to people, and to be able to set them free, moved Him to lay His hands on every single person, one by one!

It was also this earnest enthusiasm and His sincere, intensely passionate love for people that caused Him to push through (and not think of Himself first) to die on the cross, so that He could save them and have them share in the treasures of the spiritual realm and of eternal life!

Please pursue knowing God, knowing your own calling, your healing, peace and joy with the unwavering passion of a small child!

5. Be Teachable Like a Child

The Word says to train up a child in the way he should go, and when he gets old, he will not depart from it.

Even when they challenge you or throw a tantrum and you need to discipline them, a small child is very likely to receive the correction and be shaped by it. Even when they go through rebellion, one day – when the time is right – the penny will drop, and they will receive insight and be grateful for what you've invested in them.

Jesus' Example of Submitting Under Authority

When Jesus was 12 years old, He wandered off to the temple. When His parents went looking for Him after three days, He had a bit of an attitude saying, "Why were you looking for me? Did you not know that I must be in my Father's house?"

Submitting Under Authority Has Good Consequences

However, He submitted and went home with His mother, and "Jesus increased in wisdom and in stature and in favour with God and man" (Luke 2:41-52).

Being able to receive correction, to submit to authority that God has placed there, and to not be filled with stubborn pride, rebellion, and hard-heartedness are extremely valuable to grow and mature!

God, as a parent, corrects His children so that they may <u>develop everything</u> that He has planned them to be. His correction is <u>for their good</u>, so that they may <u>share in His holiness</u> and <u>produce fruit of righteousness</u> (Hebrews 12). If righteousness is a tree, what do you think its fruit looks like?

When God corrects you, it could be that you are not using what He has given you properly, or maybe you have overlooked something that is right under your nose that could give you the breakthrough... If only you would take some advice from God, or from somebody He sends along your way...

 Glory to Glory Q&A

How genuine is your love?

On a scale from 1 to 10, rate the love you feel in your heart for:

1. God
2. Your earthly father
3. Your earthly mother
4. Your spouse or person you are in a close relationship with
5. Each of your children (if you have any)
6. Your friends
7. Your enemies

Training in Godliness by the Holy Spirit

Godliness

Godliness is to be able to tap into God, and to submit under Him.

Being Led by the Holy Spirit

Romans 8:14
> For all who are led by the Spirit of God are sons (mature children) of God.

Knowing who God is and how much He wants to guide, protect, and lead you, as well as fight on your behalf, should inspire you to not even consider doing anything without His guidance!

Be led by the voice of God – either through the voice of the indwelling Holy Spirit, or by the voice of God through His Word.

God's way is the way of blessing!

Father God gives the Holy Spirit to anyone who asks Him (Luke 11:9-13).

Why Was the Holy Spirit Poured Out?

Through the prophets, God promised that He will pour out His Spirit on all flesh.

The Holy Spirit was sent to help you overcome your flesh, and to help you live ordinary, everyday life in union with the Lord.

Through the prophet Ezekiel, God declared that He will give them a new heart and put His Spirit in them so that they will be able to walk in His ways, doing His will, according to His values.

God earnestly made known His heart that He would pour out His Spirit in the hearts of people for the sake of His name, because they were dishonouring His Name.

He gave Israel His name and all the nations of the world knew that they were the Lord's people. Then they behaved atrociously, and did horrible things that the Lord said "didn't even enter His mind."

That was when He said that He would give them a new heart and put His Spirit within them.

Grieving the Holy Spirit

Israel grieved the Holy Spirit when they rebelled against the Lord's prophets and refused to listen to their correction, but stubbornly continued to reject the Lord and dragging His name through the mud (Isaiah 63:10). Jesus warns that we must not grieve the Holy Spirit (Matthew 12:28-32; Ephesians 4:30).

Your Helper and Teacher

It is very comforting to know that the Holy Spirit is our teacher who instructs us, reminds us who we are, and helps us to go where we should go.

The Holy Spirit speaks as He receives from Jesus and from Father God (John 14:26 & John 16:13-14).

As you are reading this, the Holy Spirit is at work in your life and in your heart, to help you achieve the victory, and develop the full potential of what Father God has put in you.

Your Intercessor

The Holy Spirit intercedes for you, with groanings and utterings, according to the will of God, for He knows the deep things of God (Romans 8:26-28).

Comforter, Trainer and Guide

You are safe with Him. He is a nourisher and a comforter. He will lead you to where you receive water and food – the spiritual kind, as well as the natural kind. He knows when you need milk and when you need meat.

No child can reach maturity on drinking only milk.

The Holy Spirit trains you to discern good and evil. The mature have their spiritual discernment trained to distinguish good from evil, and to determine what is beneficial and what is not.

Paul said, "When I was a child, I thought like a child and reasoned like a child. When I became a man, I put away childish things" (1 Corinthians 13:11).

Sometimes a child tests boundaries. They test what they can get away with. They test to learn what is right and what is wrong. They test to see if they will still be loved, even after they made a mistake.

Milk is for those who are still unskilled in the word of righteousness (Hebrews 5:13-14). It is for those who are still uncertain about God's intentions and His steadfast love and mercy. They need reassurance that Jesus has paid the price for their sins, and that God promised not to think about their mistakes anymore, and that nothing will snatch them out of His hand.

Jesus even told His disciples at one point, "I still have a lot more to tell you, but what I have to tell you, you cannot now bear to hear" (John 16:12).

It is the Holy Spirit who will lead you to where you need to go, to hear what you need to hear when you need to hear it. He will help you do what you need to do and encourage you to dig deep and to persevere. He is the one who will lead you to a place in the body of Christ, where you will be safe and feel like you belong.

Transformation by Regeneration and Renewal

Titus 3:4-7
> But when the goodness and loving kindness of God our Savior appeared, He saved us, not because of works done by us in righteousness, but according to His own mercy, by the washing of **regeneration** and renewal of Holy Spirit, whom He poured out on us richly through Jesus Christ, our Savior, so that being justified by His grace we might become heirs according to the hope of eternal life.

Think about this: "Regeneration is to bring about growth and new life after loss or damage."

What loss or damage have you suffered? Maybe there were old habits, coping mechanisms or hurts that damaged your heart, your life, your relationships and even your ability to believe, hope, and love.

The Holy Spirit has the power to regenerate the new life of Christ in those areas.

Clarity

Growing up, we had these portable radios that you had to tune and wangle and struggle to get a clear sound from.

The Holy Spirit gives you the clear sound, to see and hear in the Spirit.

Fountain of Living Waters

God is the fountain of living waters.

The Holy Spirit is God's river that flows from His throne, and He will help you to tap into this life-giving anointing inside you and make it bubble up from your spirit to flow out of you (John 4:10,14&7:38)!

The gifts of the Holy Spirit are the channel through which this powerful anointing of God is displayed. Every gift of the Holy Spirit is meant to flow like a river through you to serve and love others. The gift of tongues is meant to increase your own spiritual capacity to equip you to serve others more excellently.

Gifts of wisdom, word of knowledge, prophecy, spiritual discernment, tongues and interpretation of tongues are all revelation gifts to give Godly guidance and counsel to believers.

The gifts are for anyone who believes to help them live the life they were meant to live. The Holy Spirit gives to you as He wills. You might find that as you grow and mature, it seems as if you flow more in the gifts. This is not necessarily because you receive more, but because you have grown in faith and in confidence in what God has already put in you.

Gifts of faith, healing, and miracles are gifts to reveal God's glory and powerful ability to do signs and wonders, so that people may know Him and believe.

The gifts of the Spirit are all meant to glorify God, so that people say, "Wow – God is here!", and believe (1 Corinthians 14:24-25).

1. Do God's Plan Rather Than Your Own Plan

Remember how devastated God was when Israel and Judah were carrying out a plan, but it wasn't His? A man's plans are always right in his own eyes. That is why Jesus warned that the flesh has no benefit at all.

It is important to learn to discern God's voice from the voice in your own mind, your own heart, and the voice of the enemy.

Aim to Hear God's Voice as a Natural Way of Life

Aim to become natural in the supernatural, without being a pain or super weird about it. As a child of God, hearing God's voice should be like eating or being hydrated every day.

Be comforted by the fact that everyone who confesses that Jesus is the Son of God has God living in him, and he in God (1 John 4:15). If God is so close to you, it should be easy to hear His voice, right?

So, what are the hindrances and stumbling blocks that we sometimes do not hear Him correctly?

2. The Voice of the Enemy

Pushy and Impatient

In a way, it is easy to discern the voice of the enemy, for he is pushy, impatient, and always wants to rush you into things. So much so that only afterwards you realize…"Oh-oh! This is not good. It wasn't God!"

Negative Thoughts

Where do you think all those negative thoughts come from? Stop beating yourself up about them but take authority and tell the enemy to leave! I discuss your authority further down in this chapter.

To Sift You Like Wheat

Jesus told Peter that the enemy demanded to sift him like wheat, but that Jesus Himself had prayed that his **faith** will not fail (Luke 22:31-32).

Maybe you could relate with this kind of testing as the devil attacks you to test what you believe:

- He will attack you with fear to test if you <u>know who God is</u>.
- He will attack you with shame and guilt to see if you really <u>believe that Jesus took your shame and guilt</u> upon Himself on the cross.

- He will attack you with accusations of failure and hopelessness to see if you <u>know who God made you to be</u>, and if you are confident that God will make all things work together for good.
- He will attack you with thoughts of revenge and retaliation to test if you <u>know how to forgive, to pray for, and bless</u> those who insult and harm you.
- He will allure you into pride and an arrogant display of your own power and knowledge, to test how secure you are with <u>your identity as a child of God</u>. A secure person is truly at peace with who God made him or her to be, regardless of their circumstances.
- He will push you into striving and performing, to test if you are <u>confident that your Father has a plan and purpose for your life that He will bring about as you follow His lead</u>.
- He will tempt you to walk in the desires of the flesh, to test <u>how committed you are to doing God's will for your life</u> especially when it's hard.
- He could come with his lies and schemes to tempt you to <u>break your trust in the Lord and start doubting Him and His existence</u>.
- He could tempt you with thoughts of suicide to see if you're going to <u>quit on Jesus' promise of abundant life and not push back and fight</u>!

Invasion

Invasion is an unwelcome intrusion into another's domain.

You are God's beloved sanctuary, His beautiful bride. Your heart and your mind are where the enemy wants to invade and get control to mess with you. The way he gets access, is to find a place where you feel you are lacking.

"Lack" is to not have enough of something. A feeling of lack is the root cause of greed (an intense and selfish desire for something).

How the devil got into Eve's head, and got her to look at the tree and to desire it (Genesis 3:6-6), was to first twist God's words to make it sound as if she and Adam were in lack – that God lied to them (Genesis 3:4-5).

The only reason people really desire something, is when they feel they don't have enough of it – when there is a need to be fulfilled.

The truth is that "the Lord is your shepherd and you lack nothing." (Psalms 23:1) Jesus will lead you and fulfill your every need.

Philippians 4:19
>And my God will supply every need of yours according to his riches in glory in Christ Jesus.

When you pinpoint the place where you believe you have lack, ask yourself – "What has God already given me that will satisfy this need?"

Don't allow the enemy to minimize God, and God's power, in your life.

3. What is Deception?

Deception means to be misled. It is when you think and are very certain and adamant that you heard God's voice, but then afterwards, you discover that it wasn't God's voice.

Part of Spiritual Growth

Deception is part of your spiritual growth. When you feel you have never made a mistake in hearing God's voice – be careful! You might be finding yourself smack bang in the middle of deception.

Once you've gone through deception, and have a deep conviction and wow-moment of, "How on earth could I have made this mistake?", and "O dear Lord, I am so, so sorry," then you are less likely to fall into deception again, because you know what it sounds, looks, and feels like!

Usually people only realize that they've been in deception after seeing the fruit and the consequences of their "word".

The devil sometimes comes like an angel of light. Be sober-minded and smart.

4. The Lord's Voice

Will Not Contradict the Bible

The Lord's voice will never contradict the Bible.

A Soft Voice in the Quiet and the Calm

God speaks in a soft, still voice.

When you are under pressure or feeling emotional, you need to calm down first before trying to hear from the Lord.

"Yes" or "No"

The Lord gives a "Yes" or "No" check in your spirit. "Yes" is a feeling of peace, and "No" a feeling of caution to hit the break and stop.

More often than not, I experience the Lord's voice while I'm in motion, feeling a nudge from the Holy Spirit, like a guide dog leading a blind person.

Journaling

Journaling also works for me. This basically means that I write my questions to the Lord and then start writing His replies. Alternatively, I would just start by writing, "Lord, is there anything that you would like to say to me today?" As I write these words, I feel my spirit calm down and become quiet and still to be able to receive and hear from the Lord.

This takes some practice, but it's okay. Journaling is a wonderful way to hear His voice and to practice discerning the Lord's voice from your own mind and emotions. Days, weeks, or months later, you can re-read your journal and check your spirit to see what was of God, and what was not.

Don't expect God to speak volumes every day. He doesn't have to. If He just wants to say, "Hi", or, "I love you," that's okay.

Dreams and Visions

God may also speak to you through dreams and visions. A dream is simply a night vision.

There are dreams that are not of the Lord that are simply your subconscious that is processing events in your life. These dreams are usually complicated.

When God wants to speak to you through a dream, your dream will usually have one message, to give direction (or warning), healing, wisdom or encouragement.

To get better understanding about the message that the Lord is trying to bring to your attention, ask yourself:

- "Is the dream about a path or a choice I should make?"
- "Is the dream showing something in my life or heart that needs repairing, purifying or to be resolved?"
- "What solution, advice, or teaching is the Lord showing me?"
- "What encouragement or comforting picture is the Lord showing me in my dream?"

Most dreams are not meant to be taken literally. The people, places, objects and parts of your dreams all represent something in your life. They could also be symbols from the Word - for example, dreaming about a house represents your spiritual life as Jesus used this symbol in one of His parables. I am not going to elaborate further about this here as this is a very big subject and there are specific resources included at the back of the book that you might like to have a look at.

5. The Voice of Your Own Mind

Over-thinking

Be careful not to over-think everything, for Jesus promised that His sheep will hear His voice and be able to follow Him (John 10).

Isaiah said that "His words will be close to you – in your mouth and in your heart."

If you are over-thinking to hear from the Lord and trying to force it, be careful! You shouldn't be forcing anything. When God speaks, it flows like a river.

Logical and Making Sense

If you hear something that is logical or "it makes so much sense," caution! Rather wait and make sure, for these sound too much like the voice of your own mind.

Don't try to pre-empt what you think God would say. Many times, God does not say what you think He should say. You need to hear God from your spirit and not from your mind.

Get Into the Spirit

To tap into your spirit, you need to get your mind away from yourself and away from the problem and shift your focus to the Lord: pray or sing in tongues, or quietly connect with the Lord in your spirit, or worship until you feel His anointing being released. Let go of your own ideas and be willing to receive from the Lord as He wishes.

Leave the Question With Him

What I often do when I need an answer about something from the Lord, but I don't hear anything immediately, is to leave the question with Him, and carry on with life. The Lord will always answer me in some way, shape or form whenever the time is ready.

Receive Guidance

It is not possible to always hear and do correctly on your own. You may think you do, but we are all human. Be willing to be part of the Church, the body of Christ, where you can receive guidance and correction when needed.

Remember how Adam and Eve didn't have someone to help, encourage, or correct them?

6. The Voice of Your Own Heart

Sheep and Goats

There is a difference between sheep and goats. The sheep are the ones who share the same values as God, for they desire to do God's will and they tremble at and honor His Word.

Goats are those who stubbornly pursue their own agendas and who are not open to correction or guidance from the Lord. They are those who persevere in pride and rebellion, rejecting the way of the Lord.

Wounded Sheep

Wounded sheep are vulnerable to "hear" what they would like to hear, and not necessarily what they need to hear from the Lord. When you're wounded, the pain could cloud what is coming from your spirit.

This is because the wounded sheep are often blinded by their wounds for they have formed "filters" in their hearts and minds. They hear and perceive situations, and even God's voice, through these filters and "lenses", many times without even realizing it.

As you live your life journey in companionship with the Lord, He will help you see when you are not hearing Him correctly. He has promised to finish the good work that He has started – simply give Him the control to do so.

7. When Do You Know That You Are in God's Will?

You can be certain that you are in God's will when the following three things are in agreement:

- When you've received a word from the Lord, AND
- It lines up with His Word and values, AND
- Your circumstances fall into place and line up with the word you've received.

This is one of the many things that I have learned from Apostle Colette Toach (http://www.colette-toach.com).

Be careful that you are not driven by circumstances to indicate to you that you are hearing God's voice. <u>Rather be driven by the Word</u>. However, the last piece of the puzzle to fall into place is usually when circumstances line up to what you believe you have heard from the Lord.

8. When God Is Too Quiet

There is a difference between sitting quietly with God, and when He has become too quiet.

When God has become too quiet, you need to get the hint…Something is off. Something is not right and it's time to take a step back. Re-evaluate what you're busy with. Re-trace your steps.

You need to get the memo: Somewhere you went off on your own, independently from God, and need to get back to where you left Him.

9. How to Ensure That Prophecy Is of the Lord

Paul instructed that the prophetic gift should strengthen, encourage, and build up the Church (1 Corinthians 14:3-4).

What do you think God would want to build up…, strengthen… and encourage?

When receiving a word from the Lord, always ask yourself:

- What is it building up?
- What is it encouraging?
- What is it strengthening?
- Is it a word of warning or direction intended to keep a person safe?
- Are the words from the presence of God, or were they given under pressure, or perhaps given to gain acceptance or approval from people?
- Are the words in line with the values of God's heart and His Word?
- Who is the word exalting, and who does it glorify? A word from God will always glorify Him, or lead circumstances or people towards an outcome that will glorify God.

If correction needs to be given, ensure that the meek are not disheartened and that anyone who is being corrected is equipped to change their ways.

Jesus works gently with His lambs, and He empowers you to work gently with His lambs. Also, don't think for a minute that He doesn't take a stand against ravenous wolves! He cleaned out the temple with much zeal!

When giving a word from the Lord, ensure that your spirit is submitted under God and that you have sought His face first. Not in a soul encounter where you meet God in your imaginations or your emotions, but that you have had a real spiritual encounter with God in His throne room. Wait on God. Desire Him with all of your heart. Study the Scriptures.

When giving a prophecy or ministering to people, it is not about you at all. It is about them and about God. Get yourself out of the way. It is about what God wants to do in their lives to help, equip, or heal them. It is about releasing encouragement, hope, comfort, and direction from God into their lives. You cannot trust or rely on your own experiences, your own opinions, or even your own beliefs, because they might not be true.

You need to rely on and trust in God to receive pure revelation and to convey what you have received in such a way that it strengthens, equips, and builds up faith, hope, and love in the person receiving the word, for the glory of God.

The keys of the kingdom that Jesus gave to believers (Matthew 16:19&18:18) are to bind and to loose, to take away the bad, and to release the good.

In love, God wants to remove what is not of Him, and build up what is of Him (Hosea 6:5). How does one shape a horse out of a stump of wood? By removing everything that doesn't look like a horse.

Jesus appoints leaders to equip, shape, and train His people so that only Christ is left to remain standing in their hearts and minds (Ephesians 4:8-16).

Learning Through Mistakes

Making mistakes in giving and receiving words from the Lord is part of your spiritual growth. Remember that the Lord looks at your heart. The hearts of the false prophets were not pure before the Lord, for they <u>deliberately</u> set out to deceive God's people.

When your heart is pure, believe me, when you've made a mistake in giving a word, you will be face down before the Lord, seeking His guidance and help to not ever make that mistake again.

Always Be New-Covenant-Minded

Keep in mind that God's New Covenant life is for <u>Him</u> to write <u>His</u> ways on hearts and minds.

Help them to know the Lord's voice in their own life so that they are equipped to live in relationship with the Lord as God intended for them.

People shouldn't be solely dependent on others to hear from the Lord on their behalf.

10. Your Authority

Child of God, bride of Christ – the Lord has given you authority.

Your words and your prayers have power. What are you speaking and what are you praying for?

Speak to Your Mountains

Mark 11:23
> Truly, I say to you, whoever says to this mountain, 'Be taken up and thrown into the sea,' and does not doubt in his heart, but **believes** that what he says will come to pass, it will be done for him.

Speak to your mountains such as addiction, fear, depression, hopelessness and a hardened heart. Tell that mountain to be destroyed with all the faith you have from the bottom of your heart, and from the depth of your spirit and it will come to pass.

Don't Be Afraid of the Enemy

Luke 10:18-20
> And He (Jesus) said to them, "I saw Satan fall like lightning from heaven.
>
> Behold, I have given you authority to tread on serpents and scorpions, and over all the power of the enemy, and nothing shall hurt you.
>
> Nevertheless, do not rejoice in this, that the spirits are subject to you, but rejoice that your names are written in heaven."

You have power and authority over satan and all his demons. When you tell them to leave, they have to leave.

As a child of God, it is part of your spiritual journey to maturity to realize and take up your authority over evil in your life.

1John 2:13
> I am writing to you, fathers, because you know him who is from the beginning. I am writing to you, young men, because you have overcome the evil one. I write to you, children, because you know the Father.

Young men (in the spirit) are not yet fathers. To be a father who is someone whose faith and lifestyle others are inclined to imitate, you need to overcome the evil one. Don't worry – God has fully equipped and empowered you to do so!

The devil is your adversary and he does walk around to see whom he can devour and where he can cause destruction (1 Peter 5:8).

Ignoring him doesn't make him go away. When the people tried to ignore Goliath's chants and noise, he didn't just go away! No – David had to step up with **faith** in his heart and he **acted**. He **knew** that God would give him the victory, but he didn't sit under a tree waiting for God to miraculously strike down Goliath. No – David took his slingshot and with <u>his</u> one stone, **God** struck down Goliath!

Strategies

Surrender yourself to God, resist the enemy, and he will flee from you (James 4:7)!

The Holy Spirit will give you the correct strategy for your situation, which could be:

- To speak to your mountain
- Sometimes, you'll have to rebuke the devil and tell him to leave.
- Sometimes, you'll have to be still and trust God.
- Sometimes, you simply need faith that God's anointing will break the yoke.
- Other times, He'll tell you to worship while the Lord fights on your behalf.
- Sometimes, you need to find the root cause of the enemy's presence in your life, deal with it and boot him out.
- More frequently, you need to displace any lies that you believe or negative thoughts by truth from the Word.

Negative Thoughts

How has it worked for you when you tried to just ignore those negative thoughts…?

And how did it work for you when you tried to combat them in your own power? "Try some positive thinking," they said…

Listen – your battle is spiritual (Ephesians 6). You might not like it, but it is what it is.

When you tell the enemy to go, it doesn't mean that you don't have faith! It means that you are reigning with Christ!

Don't look for a demon behind every little thing either – that's the other extreme. Remember that you are the head and not the tail.

Take Possession of Your Promised Land

The Lord promised Israel to lead them into Canaan, the Promised Land. When Joshua led them into the land – guess what? They had battles to fight! Moses tells them almost 30 times in the book of Deuteronomy that the Lord wants them to "take possession of the land".

With every battle, the Lord promised to fight for them and to give them the victory – all they had to do was to follow His instructions.

You are joint heir with Christ. This does not mean that you won't have any battles to fight. Simply follow the Lord's instructions. He still fights on your behalf and will give you the victory.

Jesus promised that the person whose house is built on the rock (Jesus) will remain standing during any storm. They are the ones who not only listen to His words, but who also put His words into practice.

Releasing God's Power Through Blessing, Prayer, and Love

Jesus instructed that you pray for those who insult you and bless those who curse you. You've been given authority by the Lord to turn bad things around by releasing God's power in the lives of others!

When you speak blessing, God releases His angels and the power of the Holy Spirit to work in their lives! It's pretty powerful stuff.

No one can say that Jesus is Lord without the Holy Spirit. You are not the Holy Spirit. By blessing them and praying that God's power and will be released over them, you are doing it correctly.

Don't pray your own will and what you "think" should happen. When you do this, you are in the flesh and not led by the Spirit. Step back and give God license to be God, or decree scripture over their lives.

God lives in those who declare that Jesus is the Son of God, and they live in God. (1 John 4:15 GW)

Glory to Glory Q&A

1. Describe a time where you thought you heard God's voice, but afterwards realized that you didn't. What made you realize that it wasn't God's voice?
2. Some people are more inclined to battle negative thoughts than others. If you need to get the upper hand over thoughts and attacks from the enemy, look at the following list and see if there are any that you are battling with:
Fear, greed, shame, guilt, accusations of failure and hopelessness, revenge and retaliation, hatred, murder; pride, striving and performing, desires of the flesh, doubts, suicide, feeling of heaviness, thoughts that you'll never be able to love again, many things going wrong at the same time and you just want to give up hope and quit believing.
Now, find God's truth in Scripture, to combat each and every one of your negative thoughts.
Memorize, visualize and meditate on those scriptures to feed Jesus (He is the Word, right?) into your mind and heart and let Him fight the battle for you.
These scriptures are like the pebble in David's slingshot. Every time you hear the chant of your negative thought, like, "You are not good enough!" or, "You will never make it!" – then you tell that voice, "How dare you insult the works of the Lord like that! I come to you in the name of Jesus and today the Lord will give me the victory for the battle is the Lord's!" Then you speak that scripture with faith and let Jesus kill your Goliath dead.
Hey, God created the heavens and the earth by His words, didn't He? His words are Spirit and life!! Have some faith! Read 1 Samuel 17 if you need more faith. Then you rebuke your Goliath in your own words, fill your slingshot with Scripture, and shoot!
3. Find a quiet place and a quiet time in your day to spend time with the Lord. Be still and ask Him if there is anything that He'd like to show or tell you.
Write down in your journal what you see or sense that comes up from your spirit.

Chapter 16

Training in Brotherly Affection and Love

Love

1Timothy 1:5 (ISV)
> The goal of this instruction is **love** that flows from a **pure heart**, from a **clear conscience**, and from a **sincere faith**.

Faith without love makes a lot of noise (1 Corinthians 13:2), so it is better to learn to love also.

You might find that this chapter is hands-on, up-close and personal.

1. Loving God

This whole book is about knowing God and being able to trust Him. Everything He did to help you believe was done out of love.

It pleases Him to no end when you accept Him and everything He freely gives you.

It pleases Him even more when you trust Him. Because when you are able to trust Him and put your faith in Him, He knows that you love Him.

When you have fallen in love with the Lord with your whole heart and soul, it is easier to obey Him.

"It Is Done!"

When Jesus cried out, "It is done!" He knew that He had done everything that He had to do, to make the way for God's Kingdom, His way of life, to be established in the earth through His Church, His body.

Through His death, the curtain that separated God from man because of sin, was torn and we have an open heaven, an open door to our heavenly Father, who we may now visit and talk to any time of the day or night.

With Jesus' resurrection, He gave us the ultimate victory, as a gift – life from the spirit. This was God's ultimate solution to the dilemma of our flesh that gets provoked by fleshly desires.

He had promised that He would give a new heart and a new spirit and remove the hearts of stone so that people are empowered to follow His ways. Remember that He has given us everything that pertains to life and godliness that we may share in the divine nature. God delivered on all His promises.

He did this so that His name would be glorified. We are children of the light and God's name is glorified when we live as children of the light.

2. Loving Yourself

If God loves you, why can't you love you?

Acceptance

Embrace who God made you to be.

It actually doesn't matter what you are good at or not. Your worth is in the fact that GOD MADE YOU. He has a purpose for your life.

It doesn't matter if the world calls you retarded, or disabled, or not good enough.

There is this great magnificent mystery of how God makes all things work together for good. If we had the 1-2-3 about everything, then we wouldn't need faith, right?

But this book gives you the 1-2-3 about God's heart. His heart and soul are to love you and take care of you far beyond what you can pray or think (Ephesians 3:15-21).

It's not about "if" God loves you, it's about "because" God loves you.

Accept and celebrate the things about you that you that cannot change. You are supposed to be inimitable.

Change

Love yourself enough to accept the things you cannot change and change the things you can.

What are the things that you have control over that keep you from living the life that God intended for you to live?

Thorns

We live on a farm and there are a lot of thorns. Have you ever had a thorn that has broken off in your foot? Although your skin healed and covered it, you know it's still there the moment that you put your foot down and step on it. Unless you cut open the flesh and remove that tiny bit of thorn, it will be sore and could even fester and become infected.

Matters of the heart that have not healed properly yet work the same way. The moment someone presses the wrong button, by saying or doing the "wrong" thing, you feel it.

A New Heart

Jesus said that out of the fullness of the heart, the mouth speaks. What comes out of your mouth?

He also said that things like evil thoughts, adultery, murder, theft, sexual immorality, false witness, slander and the like comes out of a person's heart and are the things that make a person unclean. He said that every plant that was not planted by Father God will be rooted up by Him (Matthew 15:11-13&18-20).

Every time you allow the Lord to remove from your heart what is not Christ, the peace of Christ will gain more ground in your heart. When you have received inner healing from Jesus, you will know it. You will be free and at peace.

Some weaknesses will not be changed, and the Lord will simply say, "My grace is enough for you."Then you accept it and carry on with life, knowing that God's got you.

Other weaknesses we need to die to daily, and dealing with them needs to become a regular healthy habit. These are things like combating bitterness by forgiving, speaking blessing and praying for people. Or, to combat pride, judgment, and self-righteousness by looking for the beam in your own eye first.

It's like brushing your teeth to have a fresh mouth. You brush your teeth more than once a day, don't you? Why not also keep your heart and mind fresh every day? You will notice if your heart is fresh by what comes out of your mouth.

You have to remove the weeds that are suffocating the words of God's Kingdom in your heart and mind so that they bear fruit and you live victoriously and freely!

People Pleasing

People pleasing are when you were conditioned to need the approval or recognition from people, or to get people to like and praise you so that you can feel good about yourself.

People pleasing could also be because of a fear of confrontation and conflicts. So, you will rather shut up and conform than rock the boat.

People pleasing could also be about a fear of being scolded and shamed when you've had a very strict upbringing. So, you don't trust what you have received from the Lord, but compromise to gain approval from people.

This need or this fear has made people an idol in your heart, instead of having God as the main person to please in your life.

Paul asked, "For am I now seeking the approval of man, or of God? Am I trying to please man? If I were still trying to please man, I would not be a servant of Christ" (Galatians 1:10).

To serve Christ, He needs to be number one in your heart or you will always be conflicted in your heart.

When you are deeply moved by God's words, to the extent to want to adore and please Him and only Him with everything you've got, that idol in your heart will tumble down and be thrown out so fast your head will spin, and God will be placed on the throne of your heart where He belongs!!

God's loving-kindness and faithfulness have no equal in all of creation. You have heard how He has poured out His heart to take care of the ones He loves. You are safe with Him, who can harm you?

Psalm 27:1
> The LORD is my light and my salvation; whom shall I fear? The LORD is the stronghold of my life; of whom shall I be afraid?

God is the only healthy stronghold to have.

Fear of Calamity and Destruction

When you are overwhelmed by fear, it is very difficult to have faith at the same time.

Yes, you might be praying over and over again while you ask God to rescue you, or help you, or to prevent something, but do you have peace and faith while you are praying? Or are you just frantically repeating a whole lot of words…?

When you're listening to all the negative reports on the news and all the drama and the bad things that happen around you, those things will influence your faith if you let them into your head and into your heart.

But then, read and meditate about God. Meditate on how huge, magnificent and powerful He is. He turned the water of the Nile into blood. He parted the Red Sea, and He created the heavens and the earth. He is greater than the universe. Don't you think He is able to shield and protect you?

He promised that anyone who puts their faith in Him will NOT be put to shame. But you need to ASK Him. You need to GIVE Him the license to operate on your behalf.

One prayer of **faith** has great power to move God (James 5:15).

1 John 5:14
    And this is the **confidence** that we have toward Him, that if we ask anything according to His will He hears us.

God is able to supernaturally keep harm away from you like He did for Daniel when He shut the mouths of the lions. Why did God do this for Daniel? Because Daniel put his **faith** in God and believed beyond a shadow of a doubt that God could protect him.

God will deliver when you put your faith in Him, because He said He would.

Proverbs 30:5
    Every word of God proves true; He is a shield to those who take refuge in Him.

See God as a shield, a strong tower around yourself and whomever you are praying for. When God Himself is your shield, nothing can by any means break through that shield!! There are hundreds of verses in the Bible to prove this!

Envy and Disappointments

To envy someone else means that you don't believe you are good enough or that God has a plan for your life. Both of these things are lies from the pit of hell and not the truth.

You are good enough (Psalms 8&139) and God does have a plan for your life (Jeremiah 29:11, Ephesians 2:10).

Whatever your circumstances – if, for example, you feel rejected by someone you love as you are going through a divorce, or when someone else got the promotion that you felt should have been yours – with God there is ALWAYS hope!!

How many times has the Lord promised Israel that He would take care of them? How many setbacks did Joseph experience before he ended up exactly where God had promised him? Don't look at your disappointments or compare yourself to others.

You are living your life. No one else on this earth is responsible for your life except you and God.

It's time to find truth in God's Word for your life and to listen to it and uncomplicate your life by removing the stains of envy and the hurts of disappointments.

Jeremiah 29:11
> For I know the plans I have for you, declares the LORD, plans for welfare and not for evil, to give you a future and a hope.

When you read the Bible, it is evident that every single person had a purpose. Align yourself with God's purpose for your life and see what He does for you.

Jesus knew why He came to earth. He came to show the way of God's Kingdom and to die on the cross for the sins of all mankind and to be raised from the dead in order to overcome death. Soon after He accomplished that, He was taken up into heaven from where He lived to make intercession for you continuously at the right hand of the Father.

He didn't build himself a big, flashy church out of marble and stone, because He wasn't meant to do so. He knew His purpose as He received from the Father, and He did only that.

When Jesus called Paul, He told Him exactly what He should preach to whom. The Lord sent him on missionary trips and He gave Paul companions and students. Paul spent many days in prison where he actually had time to write. As it turns out, God meant for Paul to write most of the New Testament and God aligned circumstances in his life so that God's plan would be fulfilled.

The bottom line is that God's plans for you are GOOD. He wants to give you a future and a hope.

God knows which piece of the puzzle in the body of Christ He has destined you to fill. Don't sweat it. Simply follow Him.

Sometimes, while God is training you and imparting to you what He has called you for, things might look very messy and incomplete to the extent that you think you've totally lost the plot. Don't worry about it. The lives of Joseph, Moses, and Paul took a few turns before they were released to actually do what the Lord had created them to do. Also consider that those turns shaped their character, perseverance and faith.

Also, when you are at the receiving end of someone else's envy, you will realize the destructive and oppressive force that is released by such fleshy behavior. It's like they're in partnership with the forces of evil rather than with the Lord (Ephesians 5:6-17). Don't be like that. Rather bless, love and pray for others as Jesus asked.

Be imitators of God, as beloved children and walk in love (Ephesians 5:1-2).

Bitterness

When you are caught up in the wonders and glory of God, there is no time to dwell on resentment and bitterness. Uproot this thorn tree with all its stinky fruit from your heart and soul and plant beautiful seeds of prayer, blessings and love.

Show me one place in the Bible where Jesus was bitter. There is none. Jesus was too busy living and making a difference that He didn't allow Himself to be sidetracked from what He was meant to do.

God's mercy and grace is new every morning. This is a good habit to cultivate.

Guilt

For how long are you going to keep on punishing yourself for something that Jesus took the punishment for?

There is a difference between guilt and conviction. A conviction is about knowing that you did something that was not out of love and feeling sorrow and a willingness to change about it. Guilt, on the other hand, keeps you trapped in your wrongdoing by replaying the condemnation over and over again in your mind.

Either you don't know what Jesus did on the cross where He took all your mistakes, perversions, sorrows, wrongdoings and atrocities upon Himself and became sin so that you can obtain the righteousness of God (Isaiah 53), or you keep expecting punishment because you don't know God's love (1 John 2:18).

When God says that your sins are forgiven, He wipes it out as if it never happened. It's done. He is even able to make the consequences of your sin work together for good in some way or another.

Remember how Joseph's brothers treated him and sold him and told Jacob that he had died? His brothers did things that were really bad. Yet, what they did worked together for good as Joseph ended up in Egypt and eventually, he was in the position that God predestined for him to provide for and bless his family and others.

Even when things look really bad, never forget who God is, what He can do and how much He loves you.

Rejection

Do not allow the sting of rejection to define who you are by allowing it to make a nest in your heart. Keep your eyes on God.

Maybe how you thought things should happen were not the way they were supposed to happen! Maybe you were not meant to get that job, or that position, because there is something else that the Lord wants for you.

You cannot control people or circumstances. You can pray for people and release God's blessings and the work of the Holy Spirit in their lives, but you cannot make someone love you. You cannot make someone marry you and you cannot make anyone do anything, because you are not their God. It is better to submit yourself to God.

Let it be. Trust God. Release everyone who has rejected you to God.

<u>Think about this very carefully</u>: If you were meant to be part of someone's life, don't you think God would have made certain that you were? God is excellent at placing people where they should be…

Why don't you rather have faith that God will move you to where you need to be, or help you see the value of where you are…?

Sensual Desires and Lusts of the Flesh

By now, you should have received the memo. The life that God has planned for you is much more exciting than anything that the flesh can ever offer you!

You are seated with Christ in heavenly places! As He is, so are you in this world! Your citizenship is of heaven!

Your real new life is hidden with Christ in God! It's a treasure hunt!! Stop messing around with the wrong stuff and get your mind on the stuff that really matters.

Do you know the story about the turkey and the eagles? One day, an egg of an eagle ended up amongst the eggs of the turkeys. When it hatched, the little eagle thought he was a turkey and spent his childhood believing that he couldn't fly.

Then, one day, an eagle saw him amongst the turkeys and asked him what on earth he was doing amongst the turkeys.

"You were made to fly high above in the air! Let me show you who you are," said the eagle as he took the young eagle and gave him instructions to fly.

You are an eagle. Stop messing around with living the life of a turkey by stubbornly pursuing the works of the flesh.

You were made to fly by living a life led by God.

What Are You Asking?

When you want to argue and complain that you don't have or don't receive from God, step back for a second and ask yourself, "What am I really asking God for?"

The Bible says that when you ask Him according to His will, you will receive. God's will is to heal, protect, save, deliver, give hope, to strengthen faith, to build character in His children, and to show mercy and love according to His Word and His values.

The Bible also says that sometimes the Lord has a reason for wanting to test the genuineness of your faith. Let Him. When you find yourself in this situation, then push through and develop perseverance and endurance. Why not? Thereafter you will be amazed at what the Lord has done in you and you'll have more faith than you can imagine. God knows what He's doing.

The Bible also says that sometimes we don't receive because we ask silly things:

James 4:2-3
> You desire and do not have, so you murder. You covet and cannot obtain, so you fight and quarrel. You do not have, because you do not ask.
>
> You ask and do not receive, because you ask wrongly, to spend it on your passions.

Align yourself with what God values, and submit yourself to Him, and then watch what He does.

<u>Golden rule</u>: Hand over and release to God whatever you are asking Him for. Allow Him to have the remote control and simply trust Him to do what He thinks is best.

Do you know that you can trust God to do whatever is best for you, even when it's not something that you've envisioned for yourself? Trust me, you'll be in awe of what the Lord can do in your life.

God doesn't have to move fast either. Let Him be God.

Acting Independently of God

Sometimes we have made decisions and vows independently of God. Then it feels as if things in your life do not want to work out, and you simply cannot understand why.

For example, upon going through a divorce or when you've been abused, you vowed to never trust anyone of the opposite sex "ever again"; or, maybe you've made a commitment or agreement with someone outside the will of God; or, maybe you've vowed that one day when the kids are grown up, you're going to leave your spouse.

You would only get the conviction of your wrong choices and vows once you've been stuck for a while and have seen the consequences of your decisions. Repent and give the whole mess to Jesus.

Subsequently, build your relationship with the Lord and practice to hear His voice and surrender to Him. Get Word savvy. God will reward you for submitting to Him and for being willing to do His will.

Confidence

The Lord wants you to be confident in Him and confident about what He has put in you and given you to do. When you are confident, the Lord's anointing flows.

When You Have Forgiven but Still Feel Stuck

Okay, so you have forgiven everyone who has ever done you wrong but still feel stuck. You still cannot let it go completely. That uneasy feeling of wrongdoing simply won't leave.

Then you need to look at the beam in your own eye.

It is very easy to see where everyone else is missing it, or where they have wronged you. But when you take an honest look at the inside of your soul, what do you see there?

Maybe there are thoughts like, "I would NEVER have done what they did..!" or, "I'm not as bad as them," or, "I would have done it better..." or, "I still can't get over the way they treated me..."

This is self-righteousness, judgment, criticism and... pride. It is not of Christ.

Do you know where these thoughts in people's hearts are revealed the most? In marriage, parent-child and other personal relationships, where people close to them "dare" treat them "wrongly".

Sing Hallelujah when you've discovered this in yourself!!! For then you have uncovered the root cause that keeps your flesh in control: Pride.

While you're in the heat of an argument or disagreement, you are unlikely to see it, but when you think about what happened afterwards, and you look at what is in your own heart, you might be able to spot pride.

Pride has the ability to drag God's name through the mud, because if you have pride in you, you will probably hurt people.

Sometimes the best cure for pride is failure and to have egg all over your face.

Joseph was "forgotten" in prison until he had let go of his pride. Then when the Pharaoh had a dream and the cupbearer told him about Joseph, he sent for him to interpret his dream. A humbled Joseph said, "It is not me. God will give Pharaoh a favorable answer." (Genesis 41:16)

Bride of Christ, the Lord called you aside and shared the deepest desires of His heart with you. Israel had pride and they didn't realize it because their hearts were hardened. If you have a hard heart, the seeds of God's words will simply bounce off its surface and not penetrate to grow and bear fruit.

One has to receive with <u>meekness</u> the implanted Word of God that is able to save your soul (James 1:21).

Failure has a way to break open the soil of your heart so that you can receive the Word with meekness, and your love may be genuine.

3. Loving Others

When Christ rules in your heart, the love of God that flows through you to others will be genuine and seasoned with grace.

You are able to love others God's way when you've come to notice and confront your own (maybe ugly) truths.

Once you've realized how vulnerable to wrongdoing you are yourself, it's easier to have grace with another person's mistakes and yearnings.

For love is not about seeking your own way, or about being arrogant, but it's about being kind and patient and it's about thinking about others more than yourself (1 Corinthians 13).

Once you've realized that everyone is on a journey of growth and transformation, done by the Lord, then it's easier to give them the space they need to grow.

Often people already know what they're struggling with. What they don't know is how to fix it, and to reign over it, or find peace about it.

A Mosaic of People

Years ago, I made a mosaic with glass pebbles, spelling out the name "Jesus" on a wall.

I'm sure you know how a mosaic works. All the pebbles are glued and grouted side by side, bumper to bumper, close to each other, so that none of the background wall is visible anymore, only the beauty of the pebbles is seen.

While I was busy placing and gluing the pebbles, the Lord asked me, "Do you think anyone would notice if one of these stones was missing?" Immediately, I replied, "Yes, Lord! There'll be this ugly gap! An ugly hole in my picture..!"

Then the Lord said, "So it is with My body. Everyone is significant and everyone is placed perfectly to touch and be there for those around them, as well as to receive from those around them."

Influence and Impartation

What people need is the love that God has already poured out into the hearts of His children (Romans 5:5).

This is the love to be imparted and shared amongst one another.

Matthew 13:33
> He told them another parable. "The kingdom of heaven is like leaven that a woman took and hid in three measures of flour, till it was all leavened."

Kingdom leaven is God's anointing, His Word and His glory that have the power to influence how you think and act.

When the Lord changes you from glory to glory, His kingdom leaven becomes more and more in you until you are completely seasoned with Christ.

You can only give to others what you have.

If you have Christ, they will receive Him. If you have bad morals, then that is what they are going to receive (2 Corinthians 2:14, 1 Corinthians 15:33, 1 Corinthians 5:6). A little leaven leavens the whole lump.

Bride of Christ, child of God, once you realize that your life is about serving others, you will want to impart to them what is of God and not what is of flesh.

Notice what you impart into your marriage, into your children, at your workplace.

Wouldn't you like to share only the anointing of Christ, and no lusts and works of the flesh, pride or anything that is not Christ?

Wouldn't you like to be part of the solution, rather than being part of the problem where destruction, strife and greed are the order of the day?

Love yourself enough to have only Christ rule in your heart, so that He is the one you impart to others.

Uncomfortable

It's okay when you've received anointing and gifts from the Holy Spirit being imparted to you, but there could also be a time when you've received something that makes you feel uncomfortable.

For instance, you find yourself saying things that you haven't said before that you've picked up from someone, or you have thoughts of fear, lust or restlessness that you didn't have before relating to them, and it makes you feel uneasy.

You need to see the bigger picture here - this is love and faith at work in ordinary life.

The fact that what they are struggling with has been revealed to you is not for you to gossip about, but for you to help them with. You probably need to pray for them.

To remove the feeling of uneasiness, you might want to break any spiritual links that are not from Christ to remove any unwanted impartation by simply:

- Saying, "I break any spiritual ties with … that is not of You, Jesus, and I release… to You."
- Pray a blessing over them.

You are reigning with Christ. Your words have power. When you speak to break any unhealthy links, and speak a blessing over them, you are creating something in the spirit that will help both you and them to live in liberty.

God's Glory in Marriage

In 1 Peter 3, Peter wrote instructions to wives and husbands.

He starts off at the end of 1 Peter 2, describing that we have been called to follow in Jesus' footsteps.

Then he starts in 1 Peter 3 with "likewise wives" – instructing them what to do, and "likewise husbands" telling them what to do.

With the use of the word "likewise" (or "in a similar way"), he means that wives and husbands should imitate and model their behaviour on the example that Jesus set.

The Example That Jesus Set

1 Peter 2:20-25

- When Jesus was insulted, He didn't insult back.
- When Jesus suffered, He didn't threaten in return.
- He handed every situation, and every wrongdoing over to the Father's judgment, who judges fairly.
- Jesus bore the sins on the cross that you may die to sin and live in righteousness.
- By Jesus' wounds, you are healed.
- The sheep have a shepherd. They listen to His voice, as He intercedes on their behalf and leads them where they won't have lack.

Husbands and Wives

Peter instructed wives to be subject to their own husbands, and by their behaviour (without words), the husband would be changed if they didn't obey the Word.

Husbands are to live with their wives in an understanding way. In doing so, the husbands' prayers will be answered!

Incentives

Both sets of instructions, the wives to submit and not to talk much, and the husbands to understand their wives, are not really something that comes naturally to either group.

If you have anger, resentment, bitterness or puffed-up-pride in your heart, try to behave in a pure way and not return insult for insult, or manipulation, or threatening, but be calm and gentle… it's not going to work so well! You can't fake it.

To behave in a quiet and gentle way, your soul needs to be quiet, and your heart pure and tender.

Someone who feels indignant and wronged in their heart will not be able to submit, or act respectfully, or peacefully!

I have heard many men say, "If only I could understand my wife!"

Try being understanding and giving her respect when she's back-chatting you, making you feel stupid, insignificant or invisible. It will be really, very tough to remain calm and reasonable, not returning insult with insult, when you still have triggers of your own.

Being indifferent or "neutral" is not being understanding, it's an excuse and a wall to not deal with a painful situation.

Why did Peter add the incentives?

It was to get them out of their comfort zones, to deal with their flesh, and into the spirit!

Neither wives nor husbands are to live in their own strengths! Both need God's help to fulfill their instructions.

This is God's glory at work in marriage - to live, being shaped by God and transformed into vessels of selfless love.

Both husbands and wives need to resolve their inner wounds and conflicts, dig deep past their flesh, and follow Jesus' example to let Christ rule in their hearts and minds, in order to love God's way.

The leaven of Christ needs to work its way through our hearts and minds until we are completely leavened by Him.

God's Glory in Parenting

Mary and Joseph show the way of parenting God's children under the new covenant.

Parents are much like pastors who shepherd the flock by leading them where they should go, teaching them the ways of the Lord and giving them a safe place to belong where they can develop and mature.

Both Mary and Joseph received guidance from the Lord that they were going to be parents. The Lord sent an angel to both Mary and Joseph to tell them about Jesus.

When Jesus was born and the shepherds appeared, Mary "treasured the events in her heart" (Luke 2:19).

When they fetched Jesus from the temple when He was 12, she "kept it in her heart" (Luke 2:51).

Then, the Lord gave her the honour to release Jesus into His ministry at the right time when she told the people at the wedding in Cana to do exactly as He tells them (John 2:2-5).

As a parent, you need to know that God has given you children to pastor and equip in the ways of the Lord. God advised many years ago through Moses that they had to teach their children who God is. Remember what happened after Joshua died? There were generations that didn't know the Lord because the parents didn't teach their children.

So, follow the Lord's lead and listen to His voice regarding each of your children. Keep in your heart the things that make each of them unique and special, knowing that God has a plan for their lives – and it is a good plan. How on earth can it be a bad plan? Notice their gifts and abilities and notice their weaknesses. Help them to develop what they can develop and help them to accept and have peace with who they are.

We have three children and each one of them is totally unique. What works for the one doesn't necessarily work for the other. Every child needs to be met where they're at.

You need to help them discover the treasures that God has put in them and to learn to lean on Him and to know His voice. When they are under pressure, encourage them to become calm and take a moment to hear from the Lord and to follow His lead.

While they are young, you are there to impart a solid and loving foundation. You need to live what you want them to learn. Children are very clever. They see what you do, rather than listen to what you say.

It's good when they see you fail and it's good when they see you succeed. They need truth and a safe place, not a perfect place. You are not living in a Hollywood movie, you are living in real life where there are no actors but real people. Real life and real love are better. You will make many mistakes and they need to know that it's okay to make mistakes. You are not their God, but their parent. It's okay for you to apologize to them. By being real your children will learn what God's grace is about for it is only in Him that we are made complete.

Make reading the Word fun! Do your homework and teach them the truth about God.

When your children are adults, your role in their lives differs from when they are little. Give them the opportunity to grow and make mistakes. Put your faith in God, and in what you've imparted to them. Keep on loving them and praying for them.

If you should have a child who is rebellious and rejects the ways of the Lord, the Lord understands the heartache of such a situation as He experienced it with Israel and Judah of old. Be comforted knowing that the power that you have, is God's anointing that breaks the yoke and leavens their soul with mercy. A little bit of kingdom leaven goes a long way. Trust God.

I can imagine God telling His children, "If only you'll read My book, then you'll know Me and understand how much I love you and want to take care of you."

Conclusion

The Cure for Unbelief

When knowing God and having the truth of His words and the way of His kingdom written in your heart and mind, you are equipped to kick unbelief out the door and live by faith in Him!

Meditate and feed on the truth about who He is and what He can do – every day of your life.

The Cure for a Hardened Heart, Disobedience, Pride and Rebellion

If you're smart and you learn from the Word, allowing God's values, the principles of His Word and His kingdom to work its way through your heart, mind and soul (like leaven that a woman works through dough), your heart will be softened and when you allow it, pride and rebellion be removed.

When you fall in love with God, obedience is easy. It's okay to love God.

Always be willing to look at the beam in your own eye first, because it keeps you humble and submissive to God.

God's Word

God's Word is the two-edged sword of the Spirit.

On the one hand it builds up faith and Godly character in you – brick by brick, scripture by scripture.

On the other hand, it cuts away what is not of God by piercing and separating your soul and spirit, discerning the intentions and motives of your heart, bringing about liberty and transformation.

Laugh

To assess where you're at, you may use LAUGH as a tool:

L – What are you **Listening** to? Who/what do you allow to influence your life?

A – What/who do you **Adore** that takes priority in your life?

U – **Uncomplicate** your life, according to God's Word and His values.

G – Be **Grounded** in God and His Word and embrace who He made you to be.

H - Build healthy **Habits** and uproot unhealthy ones.

You should be listening to God. This will uncomplicate your life and is good for you, for the Lord keeps in perfect peace those whose minds are set on Him.

One Habit

You actually only need one good and solid healthy habit:

Know God! Follow and obey Him with all your heart, mind, soul and everything you've got.

When you do that and allow the Lord to shape the way you think and feel, then you will experience the peace and contentment irrespective of your circumstances.

Godliness with contentment is great gain.

Build up Ancient Ruins

Jesus came to heal you and set you free so that you and your children are able to "build up the ancient ruins; to raise up the former devastations; to repair ruined cities, the devastations of many generations" (Isaiah 61:1-4).

It is time for you to walk into your destiny of living the life that God intended for you to live. The life that God intended for you is a Holy Spirit filled life of blessing and contentment as you put your faith in Him, to lead you and do according to His will by living your ordinary, everyday life in companionship with the Lord.

Only the Lord can satisfy your soul, like water satisfies dry land to make it bring forth green sprouts of life. He is your Maker and the one who helps you have faith in Him.

How to Bear Fruit

When your words and actions bear good fruit, Father God is glorified, and His name is honored and lifted high.

You and I cannot make the fruit happen. The fruit is found in the vine who is Christ living in you. What you can do is to accept God's grace and rely on Christ with every breath you take.

God Has Done His Part:
1) You are GOD's own workmanship.
2) God has predestined you for what He has called you for.
3) God will protect you and get you to where you need to go.
4) God works everything together for good for those who are called according to His design and purpose.

5) God gave you His Word, Holy Spirit, and has put everything you need for life and godliness inside you, as your Manual and Helper.

(Ephesians 2:10; 2 Corinthians 5:17; Romans 8; John 6:63).

Do Your Part:

1) Submit to God and allow Him to shape you.
2) Allow the Holy Spirit to lead you, for He trains you.
3) Listen and obey God's voice and follow His lead. Do the Word. Live the Word. Apply the Word in your everyday life.
4) Be willing to submit under parents and spiritual leaders whom God has appointed and placed in your life to help and teach you.
5) Be willing to change. If the Word says that we are being renewed and transformed, it means that you need to change. Let God do it.
6) Believe God.
7) Focus daily on building your relationship with God. He is your Immanuel, part of every detail of your everyday life, wherever you are.
8) Receive the kingdom of God like a child.
9) Embrace pressure, because pressure makes you dig deep to where Christ lives in you, so that He can give you the strength and live through you.
10) Always give all the glory to God. If you want to boast, then boast in the Lord, because He made you. Everything you have, and everything that you are able to do and be, is all because of Him.

Peace, and love with faith be to God's family from God the Father and the Lord Jesus Christ. (Ephesians 6:23)

Glory to Glory Q&A

1. Think about the fruit of the Spirit for a moment: Love, joy, peace, kindness, goodness, patience, gentleness, faithfulness and self-control. Now consider who in your life has inspired you by them having any of this fruit displayed in their life.
   Is there anybody that have imparted the fruit of the Spirit to you?
2. Have you ever spent time fellowshipping with someone who has been struggling with something and afterwards you felt uneasy as the things they were struggling with appeared in your life? Things like fear, anxiety, cursing, judging, marital problems and the like?
   If so, what did you do?
3. If you are married, ask the Lord how you could pour out blessing and love on your spouse in a glorious, exciting, new way that you have never done before.
4. If you are a parent, ask the Lord how you could bless each of your children in a very special and personal way – each according to their own needs, personalities and desires - that would make them feel loved.
5. If you are neither a parent, nor a spouse, choose a friend on whom you could pour out a blessing from the Lord, in a fun and endearing way.
6. Choose an orphanage, old age home, street children or shelter on which you could pour out a blessing from the Lord.
   Do not tell anyone that you have done this. Your heavenly Father will reward you.
   Pour out a blessing on your spiritual leaders, caretakers, or parents. Notice all the many little things they have taught you and be thankful for the many big and small things that they have imparted to you.
   Simply surprise them with something thoughtful and caring, from your heart.

Dear Father, thank you for pouring out Your blessings upon this person who is reading here. Thank you for making everything in their lives work together for good. Thank you for everything. May Your Name be exalted in every life, and the love of Christ rule in every heart and mind. Amen.

Recommended Resources

1. How to Hear the Voice of God, by Colette Toach; published by Apostolic Movement International.
   Available at http://www.ami-bookshop.com or http://www.amisa-bookshop.com

2. The Way of Dreams and Visions, by Colette Toach; published by Apostolic Movement International.
   Available at http://www.ami-bookshop.com or http://www.amisa-bookshop.com

3. Shifting Atmospheres, by Dawna de Silva, published by Destiny Image® Publishers, Inc.
   Available at shop.bethel.com

4. Bible Time Line ©2005 RW Research, Inc, published by Rose Publishing, Inc.